A Hurricane of Farcicality
Donald DeMarco

A Hurricane of Farcicality
by Donald DeMarco
Copyright © 2022 by Donald DeMarco
Designed by James Kent Ridley
Published by Goodbooks Media
Printed in the U.S.A.

ISBN: 9798357600752

3453 Aransas, Corpus Christi, Texas, 78411
goodbooksmedia.com

DEDICATION

This book is dedicated to my daughter-in-law,
Frances DeMarco, whose life is a tapestry of care.

Acknowledgments

The author wishes to thank the editors of The Wanderer, The National Catholic Register, and Catholic Exchange for graciously permitting the publication of articles in this book that formerly appeared in their periodicals.

Also deserving thanks is our proof-reader, Jocelyn Pollard, whose keen eye has saved this work from many embarrassments.

EPIGRAPHS

"The 'Unity President' views his political opponents
as domestic terrorists."

(Dan Bishop R-NC in response to a Biden speech.)

"Just jump on a bus and head down to Florida where you
belong O.K.? You are not New Yorkers."

(NY State Governor Kathy Hochul
to 5.4 million NY State Republicans.)

"Every once in a while I make a mistake, like, well,
in a speech."

(President Biden)

"We're going to talk a lot about aircraft flying at sub-
sonic speeds—supersonic speeds. To be able, figura-
tively, if you may, if we decide to do it, traverse the
world in about an hour, travel 21,000 miles per hour.
So much is changing and we have got to lead it."

(President Biden)

LGTB-doctor praises 'transgender' boy for boldly
killing himself.

(News item)

"The object of life is not to be on the side of the majority, but to escape finding oneself in the ranks of the insane."

(Marcus Aurelius)

Table of Contents

"Philosophers talk about post-modernism. Political scientists talk about post-liberalism. But today we live in post-sanity America."
(H.W. Crocker III)

INTRODUCTION

In 1930, the Spanish philosopher, José Ortega y Gasset wrote *The Revolt of the Masses* in which he described the ascension of the masses to complete social power. "The mass-man," he wrote, "will not plant his foot on the immovably firm ground of his destiny, he prefers a fictitious existence suspended in air." There are many disturbing parallels between what he observed in his time and what is currently transpiring in America. What he called "the sovereignty of the unqualified" is reappearing in the United States in the form of barbarians vandalizing churches, statues of saints, memorials, and pregnancy centers, and terrorizing Supreme Court justices with whom they disagree. America has gone from claiming that marriage is just a piece of paper to the claim that the United States Constitution is just a piece of paper. Without marriage and the Constitution, however, Americans also find themselves "suspended in air".

Civilization is the concerted attempt to reduce violence to being the last resort. Today, in the United States, things have become inverted so that certain groups believe that violence will usher in a better society. Abortion is violence, and its defenders are using violence in the hopeless attempt to make it the first principle of their new society.

The present age in the United States has been dubbed "The Age of the Absurd". There is good reason for this appellation. Nonetheless, an absurdity can be recognized as such and avoided. Insanity is another thing. When the light of reason has been extinguished, insane actions cannot be recognized by insane people for what they are. They can no longer be engaged in rational discourse. America has crossed the line from "The Age of the Absurd" to the "The Age of Insanity".

Ortega spoke of "a hurricane of farcicality" that was "everywhere and in every form" that was sweeping over Europe. What he referred to may not have been as utterly ludicrous as what is now given currency in the United States: It is now possible for a "man" to give birth without becoming a mother since that term is no longer politically acceptable—"mother" and "father" (but not obscenities) are now deemed offensive. New York City has spent $200,000 of tax payers' money on drag queen shows for public school children. It is acceptable for men to compete in women's sports. People have been punished and reviled for maintaining that there are just two sexes. America's president argues that abortion is needed so that women can fulfill their God-given potential; her vice-president claims that overturning *Roe v. Wade* will be a threat to everyone; while the Speaker of the House claims that a recognition that the Constitution does not provide for abortion is an "abomination". A Supreme Court nominee could not define "woman" even though she was nominated precisely because she is a woman. Defunding the police is urged in order to reduce crime. Any word that a person does not agree with is automatically called "hate speech". The only way to respond to a "micro-aggression" is through a "macro-aggression". The family is an "out-dated" institution". Leaders of "Black Lives Matter" affirm abortions for unborn children who are black. A group of penitents gather together to apologize in a formal manner for sins they did not commit against nameless individuals who lived more than one hundred and fifty years ago.

The list goes on, but given its broad sweep and how it attacks fundamental verities, one wonders if America can go on. The natural relationship between liberty and reason has been broken. Whereas we gain liberty through reason, the current belief is that we gain liberty as we are liberated from reason. Where reason is muzzled, however, dialogue is terminated. And in the absence of dialogue, violence enters the picture. A nation cannot survive when violence becomes its first principle and its supreme arbiter.

How can a hurricane of farcicality subside so that it is succeeded by a calm after the storm? The leadership that is critically needed at this moment is actually involved in adding fuel to the fire. The mass media seems unaware of the gravity of the situation. Education remains committed to political correctness and the mantra of diversity, inclusivity, and equity, which are essentially incoherent. Nobel Laureate William Butler Yeats sized up the situation when he said:

> *Things fall apart; the centre cannot hold;*
>
> *Mere anarchy is loosed upon the world,*
>
> *The blood-dimmed tide is loosed and everywhere*
>
> *The ceremony of innocence is drowned;*
>
> *The best lack all conviction, while the worst*
>
> *Are full of passionate intensity.*

Where will America find healing except through a return to God? In the meantime, to exacerbate the situation, churches are being vandalized as people are defecting in droves. Covid-19 continues to plague people while the rate of inflation reaches an unbearable high. Yet, as the enemy reveals the uglier aspects of its plans, the more it becomes difficult to deny the evil that it represents. Naiveté is difficult to maintain in a war. Political correctness will crumble the more evident its futility becomes. God is ultimately in charge, but will He intervene without an onslaught of prayers?

"IT'S A MAD, MAD, MAD, MAD WORLD"

No. 114
Oct.
'67
MAD
30¢
CHEAP

PART ONE

A HURRICANE OF FARCICALITY

Behold Man Without God #4 by William Kurelek

THE SOVEREIGNTY OF THE UNQUALIFIED

"The sovereignty of the unqualified" is a *bon mot* that belongs to the Spanish existentialist Ortega y Gasset. It appears in his 1933 classic, *The Revolt of the Masses*. The clash between civilization and rule by the masses is a perennial problem. In his book, *Man Against Mass Society*, the French existentialist Gabriel Marcel states that:

> The masses are of their very essence—I repeat, of their very essence—the stuff of which fanaticism is made: propaganda has on them the convulsive effect of an electric shock.

America is now reeling from the thought that *Roe v. Wade* might be overturned. Hysteria, fueled by a fanatical president and media propaganda has produced a wave of fierce protests based on sheer ignorance. "We hold," Justice Samuel Alito declares in lofty Jeffersonian prose, "that *Roe v. Wade* must be over-turned.". He writes, in his 67-page statement, that:

> The Constitution makes no reference to abortion, and no such right is implicitly protected by any constitutional provision, including the one on which the defenders of Roe and Casey now chiefly rely.

On assuming the office of a Justice of the Supreme Court, the candidate takes the following oath:

> I, _______, do solemnly swear (or affirm) that I will support and defend the Constitution of the United States against all enemies, foreign and domestic; that I will bear true faith and allegiance to the same; that I take this obligation freely, without any mental reservation or purpose of evasion so help me God.

Now, if a careful and judicious reading of the Constitution reveals that it does not provide a right to abortion, so be it. Therefore, the notion, never detected for nearly 200 years, that a right to abortion is "implied in the penumbra," as Justice Blackmun claimed, is entirely spurious. In dissent of *Roe v. Wade*, Justice Byron White expressed his respect for the Constitution when he said that the decision was "an exercise in raw judicial power". *Roe* actually took away rights, namely, the right of states to regulate abortion. Justice Alito also criticized *Roe v. Wade* for "interposing a constitutional barrier to state efforts to protect human rights". Overturning *Roe* may open the way toward recognizing once again, the rights of the unborn. If anything, overturning *Roe* is on the side of restoring and not removing rights.

The hue and cry that overturning *Roe v. Wade* will take away a woman's right to abortion has no merit. That alleged right was never there in the Constitution. One cannot remove something that was never there. Instead of explaining this to the people, President Biden fraudulently claims that overturning *Roe* will embark America on a course that will remove other rights. It is far better, we can say, to overturn *Roe v. Wade* than to turn judicious interpretations of the Constitution over to ignorant mobs.

Abortion is not a matter for the Supreme Court. It is a matter for states to regulate on the basis of a democratic process that reflects the will of the people. Abortion will remain available on a state-to-state basis. As the late Justice Antonin Scalia has remarked:

> The permissibility of abortion and the limitations upon it, are to be resolved like most important questions in our democracy by citizens trying to persuade one another and return the issue of abortion to the people's elected representatives.

What, then, are the protesters protesting about? They are protesting the Constitution, its proper interpretation, and the legitimate work of the Supreme Court justices. In opposing the Constitution, however, they are protesting the very country in which they live: the United States of America, with its provisions for justice, liberty, and equality.

The Constitution is the backbone of American society. Without a backbone, society would fall apart just as the body would fall apart if it had no backbone. The Constitution provides a standard by which disputed issues can be resolved. Such issues cannot be resolved by mob protests. In the absence of a Constitution, there would be no norm by which one mob should be favored over another. The inevitable consequence of not being able to resolve issues would be violence. The United States Constitution stands against violence and for a civilized way of settling controversial issues.

Matthew Arnold, in his poem *Dover Beach*, employs the expression, "ignorant armies clash by night". His words apply to that which is currently transpiring in America. Those who are ignorant of what is happening, those who act without the light of knowledge, are not qualified to protest. They claim superiority, but lack the requisite intelligence. They represent the "sovereign-ty of the unqualified". They want to turn society upside down so that mob rule usurps the rule of law.

How Does One Converse with a "Catholic" Politician?

In our age of division, which is the sharpest of its kind in America since the Civil War, there is one thing that is commonly agreed upon, namely, that there is a critical need for social reform. However, this unanimous call for reform immediately degenerates into division when people, especially politicians, cannot agree on how to begin engineering this reform.

The beginning of any reform is the recognition and acceptance of truth. Conversely, truth is the first casualty of war. Peace demands the recovery of truth. We are now engaged in a Culture War in which we are divided about the reasonableness of accepting truth as the starting point for this critically needed reform.

The reaction among many "Catholic" politicians to the possible overturning of *Roe v. Wade* makes clear their conviction that truth must be set aside so that unreason can be given a place of primacy. Consider the reactions of the following high level "Catholic" politicians concerning the possible demise of *Roe v. Wade*. They firmly believe that partisan ideologies should overturn the very Constitution that provides America with its unifying moral standard.

Speaker of the House, Nancy Pelosi, (D-CA): "The Republican-appointed Justices' reported votes to overturn *Roe v. Wade* would go down as an abomination, one of the worst and most damaging decisions in modern history." – May 3, 2022.

The choice of the word "abomination" is curious since Vatican

II stated that "life must be protected with the utmost care from

the moment of conception: abortion and infanticide are abominable crimes." Does she now believe that it is the opposition to abortion that is abominable? How does one maintain a Catholic status given such contradictory interpretations of an important Church document? Perhaps Vatican II must be overturned, as well as all of Scripture.

Rep. Greg Stanton (D-A): "It's outrageous the Supreme Court appears poised to overturn the right to an abortion." – May 2, 2022.

There is no "right" to abortion in the Constitution. That is

the point that Alito is making. Scrutinize the Constitution as you may, it says nothing about abortion one way or another. The 1973 decision was, as Justice Byron White stated at the time, "an exercise in raw judicial power". No one saw such a "right" for nearly 200 years. Blackmun's claim that it was "implied in the penumbra" was more than a stretch. It was an unwarranted invention.

Gov. Gavin Newsom (D-CA): "Our daughters, sisters, mothers, and grandmothers will not be silenced. The world is about to hear their fury. California will not sit back. We are going to fight like hell." – May 2, 2022.

It is more than presumptuous to declare that all females oppose the overturning of *Roe v. Wade*. There are many organizations of women who strongly oppose abortion and are delighted to learn that this erroneous decision may be overturned as other bad decisions, including the *Dred Scott* ruling have been overturned. These women will not be silenced, but will cheer the Court for its courage and perception. One may fight, but, more importantly, will fighting convince?

Gov. Paul Murphy (D.-NJ): "A truly dark day in America with news reports that the Supreme Court has voted to overturn *Roe v. Wade*." – May 2, 2022.

The simple truth of the matter is that the Court is correcting a mistake. That does not constitute a "dark day". It should be regarded as a day of enlightenment. It would be a dark day if an egregious error was affirmed and perpetuated. The word "truly" is interesting since it displaces truth with a lie.

Gov. Kathy Hochul (D-NY): "For anyone who needs access to care, our state will welcome you with open arms. Abortion will always be safe & accessible in New York." – May 2, 2022.

Abortion is not a form of "care". It

is lethal for the unborn children and very often damaging to the mother both physically, mentally, and spiritually. The adverse effects of abortion on the women are well documented. Furthermore, no one can truthfully predict that all abortions, in New York State or anywhere else, will always be safe. Many other forms of care for women will remain intact for women in NY.

Sen. Dick Durbin (D-IL): "If true, this draft opinion that circulated last night would end a half-century guarantee that reproductive rights are protected by our Constitution." – May 3, 2022.

"Reproductive rights" is a sweeping term and does not include a Constitutional right to abortion. Such rights were never included in the Constitution. The point is that Alito recognized that Roe v. Wade was a mistake and required a judicious correction. Abortion "rights" were never there. Consequently they could not be taken away.

Sen. Bob Menendez (D-NJ): "In this moment, I want women in NJ and across the country to know that I will never stop fighting for your right to choose." – May 3, 2022.

"The right to choose" is based on the assumption that there is such a right. There is no moral right to kill an innocent human being, even though that being resides in the womb. "Choice" is an incomplete moral statement because it conveniently excludes what is chosen. We do not have the right to steal, loot, slander, and defame, even though such choices are often made. Moreover, the choice to abort is preceded by several other dubious choices, including the choice to ignore the humanity of the unborn, the damage to the mother, to the integrity of marriage, to the family and to society. These are all negative choices which exclude the positive choices to love, care for, and protect.

Christ is Truth. The assault on truth is also an assault on Christ. The Constitution has served the American people very well over a course of more than 200 hundred years. Its recent possible  decision should not be overturned by politicians who remain ignorant of the undeniable fact that the United States Constitution makes no provision for abortion. They should be applauding Justice Alito and his colleagues on the bench who agree with his careful judgment. A rejection of the Constitution is essentially un-American as well as a rejection of the legitimacy of the Supreme Court. No society can be deemed civilized if its founding principle is to kill. If politicians cannot accept truth, they have no business being politicians. Voters beware!

THOU SHALL NOT FOIST

Nancy Pelosi, a self-declared Catholic, has been formally excommunicated by San Francisco's Archbishop Salvatore Cordileone because of her strong and persistent affirmation of abortion. On May 3, 2022, she stated that the possible overturning of *Roe v. Wade*, would be an "abomination". In so saying, she could not have made her rejection of Church teaching more transparent. According to Vatican II, life must be protected with the utmost care from the moment of conception: abortion and infanticide are abominable crimes.

Mrs. Pelosi, however, is not without a strong moral sense. Although she does not object either to abortion or, in some instances, to infanticide, she is critical of pro-lifers who immorally "foist" their views on others. Her word "foist" is well-chosen. It means to insert or introduce surreptitiously something that is inferior or unwarranted. The following are two examples of how it can be used in a sentence: "The government has decided to foist another tax increase on the public." or, "The Company has decided to foist imperfect goods on unsuspecting consumers."

One can heartily agree that "foisting" is a bad thing and cannot be justified. Therefore, Nancy is correct to oppose it. But she is not correct in accusing pro-life advocates of this wrongdoing. In the nearly fifty years since *Roe v. Wade*, pro-life advocates have been engaged in a thoughtful discussion of abortion. One finds in periodicals such as *The Human Life Review*, *First Things*, *Linacre Quarterly*, *Ethics & Medics*, and other outlets, a fair-minded and intelligent presentation on the subject. They feature sensitive and realistic contributions from outstanding writers from science, law, sociology, philosophy, theology, and literature. These writers are not "foisting" but enlightening. We should not foist. That should go without saying. But neither should we misrepresent. Sharing knowledge is not "foisting"; it is educating. Mrs. Pelosi seems solidly against education, at least on the subject of abortion.

Meanwhile, on the other side of the ledger, pro-abortion advocates have been stuck in a quagmire for the past fifty years in shallow and irresponsible rhetoric: "my choice," "my body," "my future," etc. If there is any "foisting" going on, it is from the pro-abortion side. If *Roe v. Wade* is overturned, it will not be because the Court is foisting an erroneous opinion on the public, but simply because it recognizes that there is no provision in the United States Constitution that justifies abortion. The Court would not be guilty of foisting anything on anyone. It would simply be acting in accordance with the Constitution.

In a similar way of dodging the issue of abortion, President Biden has stated repeatedly that he would never "impose" his Catholic views on the public. In so saying, he appears to be an open-minded champion of the separation of church and state. In stating his position, however, he makes two egregious mistakes. The first is that opposition to abortion is not peculiarly Catholic. Abortion is fundamentally a humanitarian issue. "Thou shall not kill" was directed not only to Catholics (there were not any around at the time of the Old Testament writers) but to all human beings. If Biden were consistent, he would have said: "I am a human being, but I will never impose my humanitarian views on the public." And where would that leave him?

The second error is in equating service with "imposing". To "impose," in Biden's use of the term, means to force upon someone that which is not welcomed ("The decision was theirs and not imposed by others."). One does not impose, however, when he assists in securing what people need. In this sense, he is not imposing, but serving or ministering. Not to know the difference between "imposing" and "serving" should disqualify anyone from public service. It is most unfortunate that this distinction is lost on the president of a country.

I recall debating Eleanor Pelrine, a staunch pro-abortionist who had written a book on Canada's most prominent (and notorious) abortionist, Henry Morgentaler. During the debate, I cited the *Wynne Report*, an extensive report on the medical knowledge

available at the time culled from leading medical journals. The report, issued in Britain by highly respected researchers, was neither pro- nor anti-abortion. But the researchers recommended that, given its many adverse consequences, abortion should not be obtained unless the woman has completed her family. According to Mrs. Pelrine, the *Wynne Report* had been refuted by the *Shadd (?) Report*. I thought it was exceedingly odd that one report could negate all the scientific findings of a myriad of highly respected medical journals representing several countries. I told her that I was unfamiliar with such a report and asked her if she would be kind enough to send me a copy. She promised to do so, but I was not hopeful. The years have passed and Mrs. Pelrine has left the stage. My chances of ever receiving a copy of that mysterious report are not looking very good. Had I thought of it during the debate, I could have said, "Oh, the *Binge Report* has refuted the *Shadd Report*." I think I was "foisted upon" by a reference to something that never existed.

In order to maintain a pro-abortion position one must resort to chicanery and projection. First, attack the opponent with hollow rhetoric; secondly project you own inadequacies onto them. In this way deceit triumphs over enlightenment. Pelosi and Biden have pulled the wool over the eyes of many Americans. In Pelosi's case, her excommunication is because her position on abortion is hostile to Catholic teaching and a scandal to Catholics. But underlying that, she is excommunicated from the citizenry of rational beings insofar as she is guilty of rejecting reason. And here is one of the tragic consequences of abortion, that the attempt to defend it ultimately causes one to lose his mind.

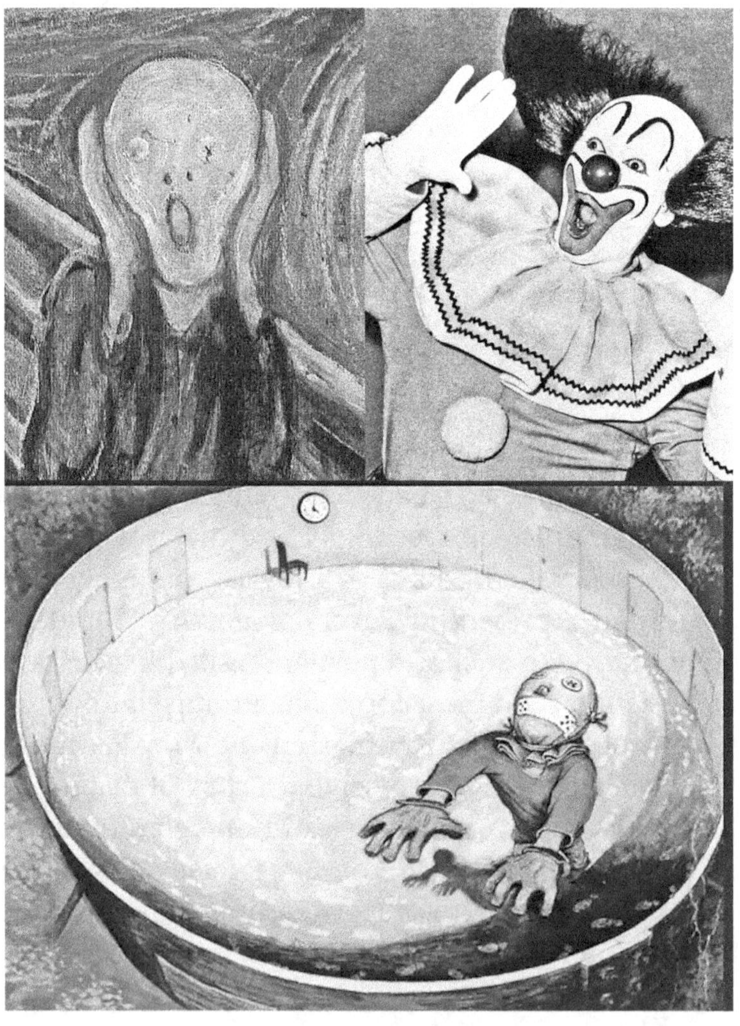

Murder, Mayhem, and Moral Myopia

We are repeatedly advised that what we eat, drink, and breathe are either beneficial or harmful to our bodies. As sensible consumers, we take this advice seriously. Therefore, we avoid bad cholesterol, high sugar drinks, and protest against air pollution. By the same token, we are told that what we see, hear, and read are either good or bad for our souls. In this case, however, we do not take the advice very seriously at all. Therefore, not always acting as sensible people, but acting in accordance with our freedom of choice, we view salacious material, listen to acid rock, and read trashy novels. But, what we put into our minds does not stay in our minds but eventually expresses itself in our actions.

People of religious faith have always understood that good music, fine literature, and beautiful architecture are important factors that properly shape our souls. And it is through the soul that our behavior is shaped. We can be obsessed with physical fitness, but neglectful of our soul in which our moral attitudes are formed. We think, naively, that the philosophy beyond abortion can be contained and not spill over into society. We fail to realize, however, that we live, not in a culture of freedom, but in a culture of death. And we are shocked when death strikes in unexpected and horrific ways. There is no greater enemy to freedom than unexpected, tragic death.

On April 20, 1999, two students at Columbine High School in Columbine, Colorado, murdered 13 people (12 students and one teacher) and wounded 20 others, before turning their guns on themselves. What could the world make of such a tragic event?

How could it possibly happen, especially in an upscale community?

At least four of the victims were Catholic. Denver Archbishop Charles Chaput promptly responded to their families to offer counseling and condolences. He remained in touch with the parents of at least one of the victims for several years afterward. Soon after the tragedy, on May 4, 1999, the good bishop testified before the United States Committee on Commerce, Science, and Transportation. He expressed his conviction to the Committee that people in society are not being taught to value human life:

> When the most dangerous place in the country is a mother's womb, and the unborn child can have his or her head crushed in an abortion, even in the process of being born, the body language of that message is that life is not sacred and may not be worth much at all.

Unfortunately, his words were not taken with the seriousness in which they were delivered or put into practice. Columbine has become a byword for more school shootings and since that time, culminating in the recent unspeakable tragedy in Uvalde, Texas that claimed the lives of more than 20 children and two teachers.

Society prepares the crime, the criminal executes it. Yet it is difficult for people to connect the dots. The alleged "right" to kill the unborn breeds an attitude that spreads throughout culture, poisoning the atmosphere, as it were, and undermining the view that all human life is sacred. Pernicious ideas that float on the wind find entrance points into the minds of the young. As the distinguished American sociologist, W. E. B. du Bois has stated:

> The chief problem in any community cursed with crime is not the punishment of the criminals, but the preventing of the young from being trained to crime.

While no direct link can be made between abortion on demand and the shootings at any one particular school, it stands to reason, nonetheless, that a disregard for the value of the life of the unborn will extend to a diminishment of the value of life of everyone. Abortion cannot remain as merely abortion. In referring to abortion, novelist John Updike has remarked that "Death, once invited in, leaves his muddy boot-prints everywhere". Abortion affects the mother, marriage, the family, and the whole of society.

We live in a Culture of Death, which means that death is not localized, but is omnivorous. Saint John Paul II has clearly expressed how death permeates culture:

> Whoever attempts to destroy human life in the womb of the mother, not only violates the sacredness of a living, growing, and developing human being, and thus opposes God, but also attacks society by undermining respect for all human life.

In *The Gospel of Life*, he tells us that:

> The acceptance of abortion in the popular mind, in behaviour and even in law itself, is a telling sign of an extremely dangerous crisis of the moral sense, which is becoming more and more incapable of distinguishing between good and evil, even when the fundamental right to life is at stake.

Abortion cannot be confined to the closet. It is more than

an act. It is the approbation of a philosophy that disregards the value of human life. As a philosophy, it spreads its contagion to other areas of life including suicide, euthanasia, and outright murder. If the well is poisoned, all who drink from it are affected, one way or another.

One cannot disrespect some human life without disrespecting all human life. This is a most reasonable point. Our society, dedicated as it is to unlimited abortion fails to see this. It is blinded and muzzled by political correctness that has created arbitrary values as a substitute for real values.

Murderous mayhem will continue to be facilitated as long as moral myopia prevails.

The Triumph of Death by Bruegel

Echoes from the Past

"Days of Rage," which has characterized the extended riots in Seattle and in other American cities, was borrowed from the riots of the late sixties conducted by the SDS (Students for a Democratic Society) and its faction, The Weathermen. Why the rage? Many of the radicals in both instances came from affluent families. And why is the rage expressed in violent terms? These are questions that many have pondered, though their pondering has produced few cogent answers.

Thomas Powers has given us a thorough inspection of the SDS movement in his book, *Diana, The Making of a Terrorist*. The author uses Diana Oughton, daughter of a well-to-do family in

Dwight, Illinois, as the centerpiece for other depicting students on the periphery who came to believe that violence was "the only way". Diana's mother tried to talk her radicalized daughter into leaving the Weathermen. "But honey," she warned, "you're only going to make things worse. You're only going to get yourself killed." "It's the only way, Mommy," Diana firmly stated. "It's the only way."

Violence proved to be both her mother's prophecy and Diana's own undoing. Shortly before noon on March 6, 1970, an explosion tore through the front wall of a century-old townhouse in New York City. Diana and three of her co-workers were its tragic

victims. The Assistant Chief Inspector of the investigation offered the simplest and least emotional explanation of what had taken place: "The people in the house were obviously putting together the component parts of a bomb and they did something wrong."

"He who lives by the sword, dies by the sword" (Matthew 26:26-52). Diana and many of her colleagues had come to hate affluence. "Kill all the rich people," ordered one of the SDS leaders. "Break up their cars and apartment". But they also hated poverty. Whatever correctives of poverty might await on the distant horizon required a realistic plan, ingenuity, patience, and above all, time. But the radicals could not wait. Their demands were "non-negotiable" and they wanted immediate results. Like their predecessors of the French Revolution, they wanted to change everything in all spheres of life with a single blow.

Violence becomes the last resort when one has despaired of everything else. It rises from a despair of life as it is, given its

imperfections and the difficulties inherent in improving its condition. Despair, however, is the inevitable path to death. The Weathermen emphasized "any kind of violence, directed at any target, under any circumstances". One revolutionary called his

34

comrades to emulate Captain Ahab in *Moby Dick* and "bring down the white whale". Ahab, of course, was not a worthy role model since he was destroyed by the white whale. The Weathermen became targets of their own misguided ideology.

The president of Greater New York Black Lives Matter has warned that if the movement fails to achieve meaningful change during its nationwide protest, it will "burn down the system". A co-founder of Black Lives Matter Toronto, a black Muslim named Yusra Khogali, has argued that white people are "recessive defects" and mused about how their race could be "wiped out". She has called Prime Minister Justin Trudeau "a white supremacist  terrorist and has urged crowds to "rise up and fight back".

The SDS and BLM share a contempt for the traditional family. They do not believe that the family is the basic unit of society. But in their revolutionary aspirations, that begin and end with violence, they have no proposal for its replacement. They dismiss the concrete and place their idealism in the abstract. This is a

Marxist philosophy that is totalitarian in its essence.

Patrisse Cullors, one of Black Lives Matter's co-founders, has been widely reported as saying that "We are trained Marxists".

The implementation of Christianity begins with love for one's neighbor. This is the irreplaceable ground from which all good things arise. Charity begins not at home but even before the home is established. In fact, it is the form which gives the family its personal satisfactions and preparedness to contribute to society. If one begins his revolution in the world of abstractions, he leaves the home in ruins. And this is the legacy of the SDA.

Whittaker Chambers recounts in his book, *Witness*, an incident that took place while he and Harry Freeman, a dedicated Marxist/Communist, had while walking together through New York's Bowery. A shivering derelict approached them and asked for a handout. Harry glanced past him, which was the proper communist attitude. To give alms, what Christians hold to be a corporal work of mercy, according to Communist principles, is to dull the revolutionary spirit of the masses. Chambers gave the wretched man what change he had in his pocket. Harry Freeman drew Chambers aside and said, "We can't save them. They are lost. We can only save our generation, perhaps, and the children." In that unheralded incident lies the unbridgeable gulf that separates Christianity from Communism.

I recall listening to a call-in radio show on the theme of how one should live his life. The special guest that evening was a philosopher who was trying to reconcile his Catholicism with Marxism. A woman called in and talked about being attentive to the needs of her neighbors and how, on certain occasions, she would bring a casserole to someone who was sick. The philosopher was critical and reprimanded the woman for lacking "social consciousness". He believed that the genesis of social reform lies in a revolutionary change in social structures. Love, as a revolutionary from the 60's once stated, is "debilitating and counter-revolutionary".

Christianity is eminently realistic because it is grounded in the love between one person and his neighbor. For the revolutionary, this is too slow, too tedious, and too uncertain. But the way of atheistic revolutions is doomed. It does not breed children, but fosters violence. We must continue to re-learn this simple and indisputable truth.

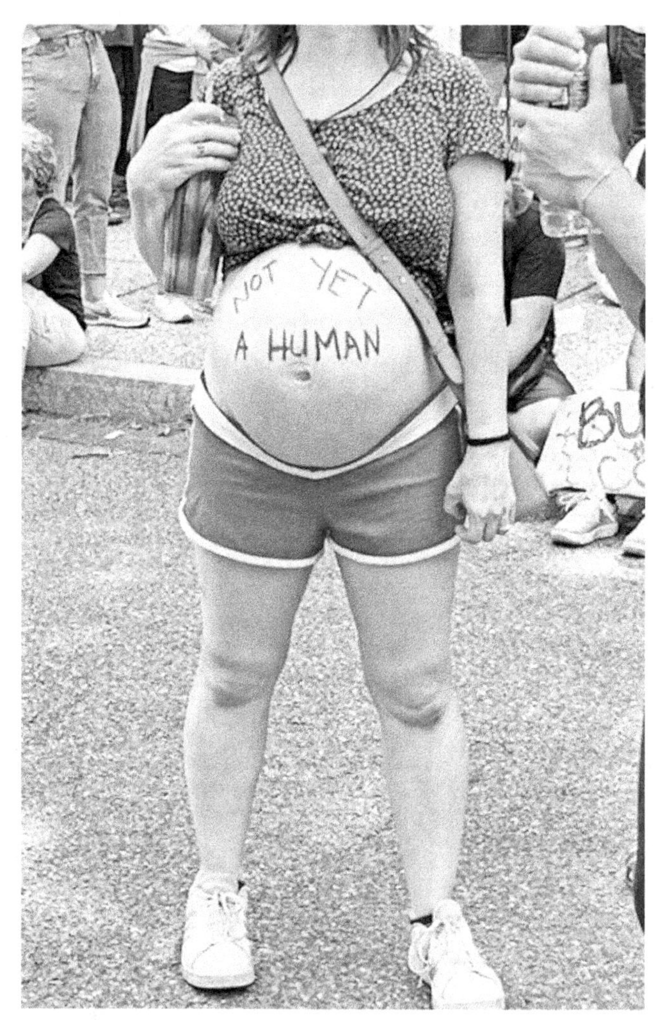

NOT YET
A HUMAN

THE PREGNANT WOMAN AS A SOLO ENTITY

Tuesday, March 8, 2022 was International Women's Day. It was incumbent on America's 46th president to salute women throughout the world and to offer them something encouraging and uplifting. He told half the population on the planet that women cannot "live up to their God-given potential" without abortion-on-demand.

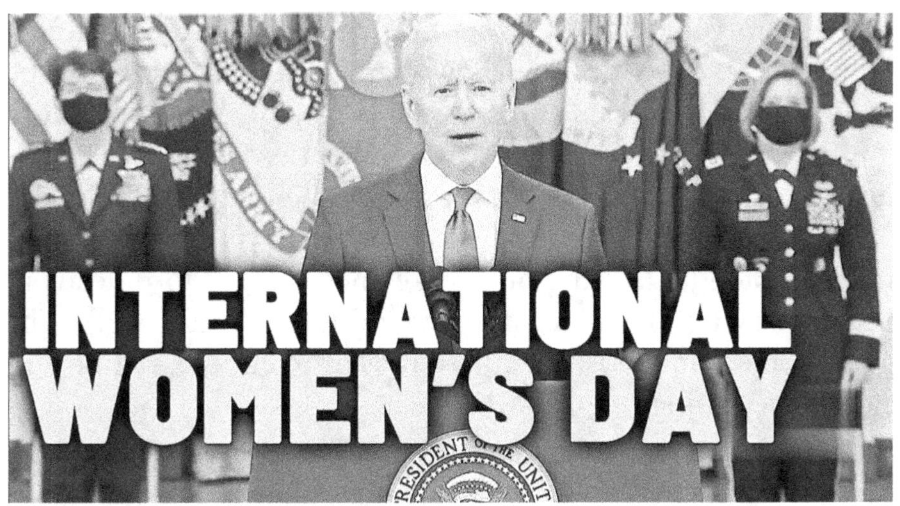

The inclusion of a reference to God is curious since hardly a week had passed when President Biden declined answering the question, "When does life begin?" by stating that he did not want to go into that "theological" issue. The beginning of life, of course, is not simply theological. Science has made it sufficiently clear that human life begins at conception when a sperm penetrates an egg to form a new organism with all the DNA it will ever have. Apparently, Biden is willing to refer to God not as a Creator, but as being unconcerned about the lives of unborn human beings that are also "God-given".

Perhaps the most outrageous of his sleight-of-hand rhetoric is his misuse of the word "potential". President Biden is not really a fan at all of potential. If he were, he would respect the potential of the unborn which is far greater than the potential of the pregnant woman. This potential includes the potential to keep on living, one that Biden regards as lacking any moral value.

Moreover, living up to one's full potential is a myth. No one has either the time nor opportunity to actualize all of his potential. By following one line of potentiality—being a writer, for example—excludes a vast array of other options. Every choice necessarily excludes what it does not include. One cannot be married and single at the same time. The difficulty in choosing marriage, often times, is how many potential mates will be excluded. Neither can one simultaneously be a mother and a non-mother. One may have a rich potential for service in the military or as a layman. But choosing one excludes the other. Trying to achieve the unachievable, namely, trying to develop all of one's potential (having one's cake and eating it too), leads to insanity (trying to get an infinite world into a finite head). The great problem in life is to figure out what to choose, not how to choose everything.

Biden demeans the rich potential of the unborn for the mere

limited potential of the pregnant woman. An adage comes to mind about a woman who owned two chickens. When one fell ill, the woman killed the second in order to make chicken soup for the one who was sick. In her myopia, which caused her to neglect the needs of the second chicken, she over-estimated the importance of the health of the first, while under-estimating the very life of the second.

The adage, naturally, is a joke. And as a joke, its folly is recognized immediately. For reasons unfathomable, Biden does not see the folly of killing one human being, with virtually all of its potential hanging in the balance, in order to preserve a more limited potential in another human being. The fact that Biden is blind to his own nonsense is one joke layered over another. An adage, thinking of chickens, one of Italian origin, comes to mind: *Non facciamo ridere i polli* (Let's not make the chickens laugh).

And then, with all women presumably demanding the "right" to abort, there is the moral disappearance of the father. Biden misses the most important moral feature of human society, namely, that it is organic. Wives need husbands, husbands need wives, children need parents, and parents need children. Fathers are essential to the organic unity of both marriage and the family. To remove the pregnant woman from the web of human relationships is not to praise her, but to isolate her and deprive her of fulfilling potentials that she could not fulfill otherwise.

A woman has the potential to be a receptionist, a waitress, or a cleaning lady. These occupations are vitally needed in society and should not be demeaned. Not every woman can become a princess. There have been precious few Grace Kellys in the world. But if a woman aborts so that she can fulfill any one of these occupations, then, a serious question arises. Why would a woman choose to be the same thing to everyone (as a waitress is) when she can become everything to her child: a nurse, a protector, a teacher, a guide, a source of nourishment, a life-long friend, and an ambassador of love?

Biden's enthusiasm for abortion logically, although retroactively, extends to his own mother. What better potentials would Mrs. Biden have fulfilled had she chosen to abort little Joe rather than giving birth to a future president of the United States? Perhaps she could have gained a prominent position with Planned Parenthood, or served as a reporter for CNN! Biden's enthusiasm for abortion appears to be stronger than his enthusiasm for his own life.

How is it possible, for the Commander in Chief of the of the world's richest country to utter such unmitigated nonsense while maintaining a smile? This is truly surrealistic! How can he possibly believe what he says concerning abortion?

Abortion, as an act of removing something that should be there, is not limited to the unborn child. It has an insidious effect on the pro-abortionist to the point that intelligence, which should guide one's thinking on moral matters, is seriously impaired or entirely removed from one's mind. President Biden, in this sense, has self-aborted. This is the tragedy of consistently following a path that begins with approving the killing of innocent human beings. President Biden, himself, does not appear to be living up to his own "God-given potential" to be a good president. His words on International Women's Day are nothing more than a travesty.

The Problem With the Potential

The word "potential" is mesmerizing. It conjures up a dreamland in which one can become anything he wants to be. It has not yet crossed into the realm of the actual where it loses its unsullied attractiveness. A young woman yearns for the perfect mate. She can maintain this yearning as long as it remains in dreamland. When she marries, she may have found a fine husband, but he inevitably falls short of the potential ideal mate who existed in her imagination. The actual

never quite lives up to the potential. Author Erica Jong said that she decided to keep her womb empty and full of possibilities. But a mere possibility is not a reality and therefore can be of no benefit to anyone.

It has become well-known that certain feminists have chosen abortion in order to fulfill their potential. A high-point in selling this idea was enunciated to the world on Tuesday, March 8, 2022 on International Women's Day when President Biden stated that a woman cannot "fulfill her God-given potential" unless she has access to abortion-on-demand.

Biden, in his enthusiasm for promoting abortion, overlooked the God-given potential of the unborn child. Nor did he consider the rights and obligations of the child's father. The pregnant woman was removed from the web of human inter-relationships and treated, rather unrealistically, as a solitary being, a "solo entity" as Professor John T. Noonan, Jr, has characterized her.

The notion of the potential is too broad to serve as a moral category. We all have the potential for any number of crimes and follies. We should distinguish between the potentials that will benefit us from those that will be injurious to us. Fulfilling one's potential is a highly ambiguous expression. The question arises: How do we distinguish between the good and the bad potentials?

First, we must replace the word "potential" with the word "inclination". We all have plenty of potential, but what we need to affirm and develop are our "God-given" inclinations. Fulfilling any potential whatsoever is not exactly a humanizing activity. To become a tyrant fulfills a potential, but it does not affirm and develop an inborn inclination. It is in being faithful to our inclinations that we are humanized. Our inclinations are precisely the potentialities that should be actualized. They define who we are.

We come into a world with an inclination toward life, a characteristic often referred to as a "life-preserving instinct". This inclination is evident in the activities of all animals. In the absence of this inclination, human beings, as well as all other animals, would be inert, indifferent to choosing one thing over another. In the words of Jacques Maritain:

> Any kind of thing existing in nature, a plant, a dog, a
> horse, has its own natural law, that is, the normalcy
> of its functioning, the proper way in which, by reason
> of its specific structure and specific ends, it 'should'
> achieve fullness of being either in its growth or in its
> behavior.

Another inclination, readily observable in babies, is to love and to receive love. Sigmund Freud, despite his many errors, had a genuine insight into the human condition when he stated that wealth does not make a person happy because it does not fulfill an infantile wish. A toddler, at his early age, has no desire to be rich.

We are also born with an inclination toward justice. A youngster playing a game will be quick to point out that his opponent is cheating. "That's not fair," he will protest vehemently. By insisting that the game be played fairly, he is being true to his natural inclination for justice.

We also have a natural inclination to seek truth and to know God. In general, we have a natural inclination or disposition to do good and to avoid evil. This deeply significant point is missing from naïvely fulfilling any potential whatsoever.

St. Thomas Aquinas uses these natural inclinations to organize the Natural Law which is the objective basis for morality. The Natural Law is consistent with the fundamental structure or design of the human being that is a kind of blueprint for his authenticity.

According to the Natural Law, the killing of an innocent human being, which takes place during abortion, is an activity rooted in one's potential activities, which contradicts the basic inclinations of both the mother and the unborn child. Motherhood, in a given instance, may very well be the fulfillment of the inclination to love. To abandon one's motherhood through abortion in order to fulfill certain potentials that are contrary to the Natural Law is the very essence of immorality.

We are dynamic creatures. Our natural inclinations are impulses or directives that help us to know who we are as loving, life-affirming, truth-seeking and God-aspiring beings. Whereas the range of natural inclinations is much smaller than the range of possibilities, it is the former which constitutes what we need. The latter can be a temptation to be what we are not

THE BROAD AND NARROW WAY.

46

meant to be. Our inclinations define and describe us; our potentialities can lead us astray. In addition, the Natural Law provides the basis for our fundamental moral rights.

Numberless women have undergone induced abortion so that they could actualize other potentialities. But contravening the Natural Law, which essentially prescribes who we are, cannot be a path to improving one's self. The Natural Law cannot be rejected for something for which we have no natural disposition. This helps to explain the well documented fact that a significant number of women experience deep regret after they have had an abortion.

It is profoundly sad that the current president of the United States seems to know nothing about the Natural Law while promoting the ascendance of the potential over the natural. The notion that "anything goes" is, in the final analysis, self-destructive. Life is not a game. It has specific rules that are built into the fabric of the human being. These rules, so to speak, are the specific natural inclinations that dispose and urge a person to become fulfilled in a way that is in accord with his God-given destiny.

The Attempt to Banish Nature

The central irony of feminism, which was founded in the interest of giving due respect to the special gifts of women, has logically led to the denial that there is such a being as a woman. "I understand," writes feminist Julia Kristeva, by 'woman' that which cannot be represented, something that is not said, something above and beyond nomenclature and ideologies." Gender studies Professor Rebecca Jordan-Young, author of *Brain Storm: The Flaws in the Science of Sex Differences*, states that there is not even a singular biological answer to what is a female. Another gender expert, Sarah Richardson, author of *The Maternal Imprint: The Contested Science of Maternal-Fetal Effects*, argues that science cannot settle what are really social questions. According to these "experts," human sexuality is no longer anchored in nature. It is now free-floating, definable by extrinsic factors.

Supreme Court Justice nominee, Ketanji Brown Jackson, caused a stir during the Senate hearings in late March when she stated that she could not define the word "woman". In pleading ignorant to something that human beings have understood for milennia and what biology has confirmed, she chose to conform to an ideology that is now suppos-

edly independent of nature. DNA, X and Y chromosomes, and genitalia are no longer relevant in defining a woman. Somehow, in ways that are not exactly clear, ideology has displaced nature. This creates the impression that we now have the power to change human sexuality and turn it into what we would prefer it to be. It is as if the science of astronomy were to regress back to the superstition of astrology, a pseudo-science for star gazers who were fond of inventing fascinating myths. The Bible, the testimony of human beings throughout history, along with what were once thought to be enlightening works, such as Pope St. John Paul II's 130 allocutions on the *Theology of the Body*, have now been superannuated. Both woman, as well as man, are now presumed, according to the *Zeitgeist*, to be above nature and not determined by it. In this way, nature is seen as having been a limiting factor that must be banished. Man (the human being) is no longer the "quintessence of dust". He has shaken off the "dust" and is, finally, what he wants to be. Or is this merely an illusion?

Chemistry, for the ancient Greeks, did not deal with 92 natural elements, but with a mere four: earth, air, fire, and water. Yet there was an added mystery to their primitive science. They believed that the stars were composed of a fifth element, or a *quinta essentia*, a higher kind of matter, immortal and imperishable. This fifth essence was the substance of the stars.

Shakespeare, who was more than willing to define what a "man" is, brought this fifth essence down to earth. The unity of this higher matter with dust constituted the nature of the human being. As Hamlet declares:

> What a piece of work is man! how noble in reason!
> how infinite in faculty! in form and moving how
> express and admirable! in action how like an angel!
> in apprehension how like a God! the beauty of the
> world! the paragon of animals!

And then, to bring his panegyric to a climax, he defines man as "the quintessence of dust".

This marvelous expression is a synthesis of starlight and earth-dust, the eternal and the ephemeral, spirit and body, the heavenly and the natural. Man is a paradox. He is not just one element, either merely social or merely natural. This is why man (including woman) is challenging both to define and to put into practice. Throughout history the pendulum has swung from one side to the other. Is man simply natural and should not be restricted by moral norms? Or is he angel, and should not be held back by his body? It is easy to define something that is simply one thing, like hydrogen or helium. But the truth of man is best expressed in a paradox. Carl Sandburg tells us that:

> Truth consists of paradoxes and a paradox is two facts
> that stand on opposite hilltops and across the inter-
> vening valley call each other liars.

Man is an enigma, claiming to be either the special creation of God or the accidental product of chance. His ancestry is either sovereignty or slime. The ability to integrate celestial aspirations

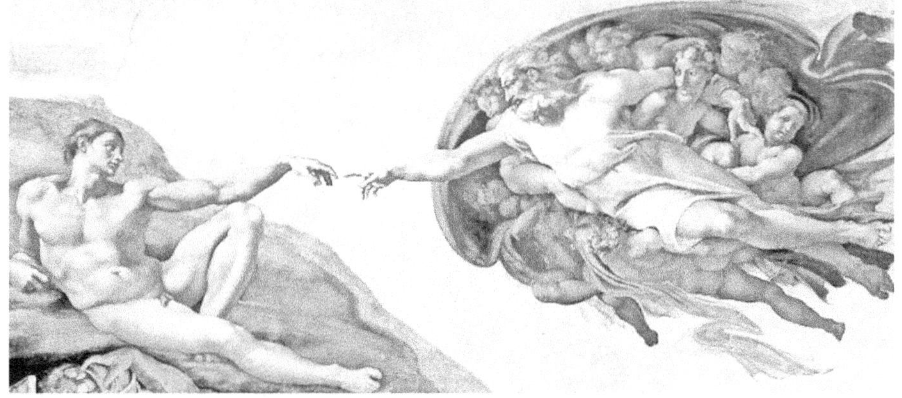

with corporeal responsibilities has long been a source of frustration, confusion, and one-sidedness. Venerable Pope Paul VI's encyclical *Humanae Vitae* was widely misunderstood because it was based on a "total vision" of man, combining the spiritual with the corporeal. The human being is a psycho-somatic entity, an integrated person.

Nature may be denied, but it will not go away. Sociology cannot supplant biology. As Cicero stated long ago, "Custom cannot conquer nature; indeed, nature will always conquer her" (*Numquam naturam mos vinceret; enim ea semper invicta*).

No small amount of humility is required for a person to accept the fact that he is an embodied spirit. It is not that the body limits us. It is, in fact, an essential factor in defining us. We are not "liberated" when we reject the body and seek a more lofty reality. As the poet Hyde Partnow has said, "I am free not because I can fly, but because my feet touch the ground." We are liberated when we guide our life through the light of reason. Reason, like nature, endures and will persist despite repeated attempts to ostracize it. Pride was the cause of original sin because our primal parents wanted to be more than they could be. Pride begets a fall because it throws away the ladder that connects us to reality.

We must re-learn what it means to be male and female. And this learning process requires little more than the restoration of common sense. The attempt to banish the body will prove, in the end, to be counterproductive.

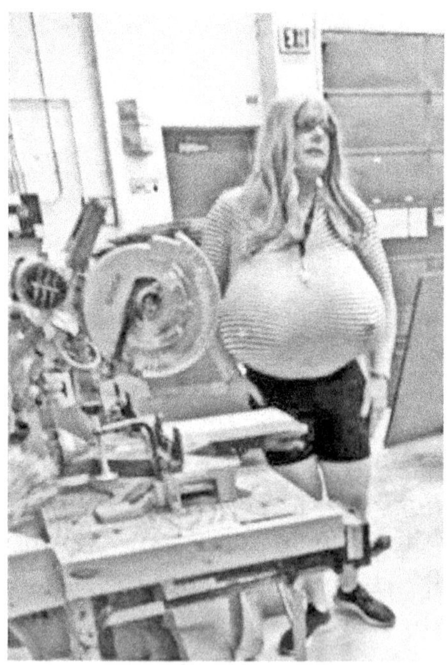

WE ARE CUTTING OURSELVES OFF AT THE ROOTS

C. S. Lewis received a complimentary copy of a textbook intended for "boys and girls in the upper forms of school". He was grateful for the gift but found the philosophy contained therein so sufficiently unsound and potentially damaging to students that he wrote *The Abolition of Man* as a corrective. The egregious error that the authors make is that they deny man's natural and spontaneous response to a world they did not create. For example, they state that when a person refers to a beautiful waterfall as sublime, he is not making a remark about the waterfall, but only his own feelings —"I have sublime feelings". In this way, the authors deny the human capacity to make realistic comments about the outside world. We are thereby isolated in our own feelings and are unable to describe anything outside of ourselves with any degree of objectivity.

For Lewis, it is an outrage that the authors of what he calls, *The Green Book*, can consider themselves educators. If we lose the power to describe a beautiful waterfall as sublime, how can we proceed to say anything more about the real world? Lewis regards this amputation of a basic faculty as being of dire importance. "We remove the organ and demand the function," he writes. "We make men without chests and expect of them virtue and enterprise. We laugh at honour and are shocked to find traitors in our midst. We castrate and bid the gelding to be fruitful."

In 1947, when Lewis penned his mini-classic, he probably did not think that the withdrawal from reality he describes would lead to the inability to recognize that there are two sexes, male and female. His thinking, however, was on the mark, and the process of eating away at objective reality has continued apace.

Jorge Cardinal Medina Estévez comes with impressive cre-

dentials. He served as Prefect for the Congregation for Divine Worship and the Sacraments, was a *peritus* at the Second Vatican Council, and has been a professor of theology and metaphysics at the Pontifical Catholic University of Chile. He begins his most timely book, *Male and Female He Created Them*, with simplicity and eloquence:

> No human institution is so deeply rooted in nature and in the heart of man and of woman as marriage and the family. Prior to any philosophical reasoning, men and women know that they are made for each other, that they need each other, and that there exists between them a relationship that is different from all other relationships found in human society.

What I want to call particular attention to is the phrase, "prior to philosophical reasoning". We do not begin with reason. Reason comes later. Our ability to respond to the wonders of creation and perceive particular realities and relationships is spontaneous. We are rooted in nature and respond to it naturally. We enjoy a kinship or affinity with nature. We are not alien beings. St. Thomas Aquinas referred to this spontaneous response and the knowledge so derived as "knowledge through inclination" (S.T. I-II, 94, 2). Before we can stand back and figure things out, our natural inclination grasps things spontaneously. We are inclined to the good. We respond to beauty prior to examining it rationally.

Jacques Maritain elaborates on this point when he states that this "kind of knowledge is not clear knowledge through concepts and conceptual judgments; it is obscure, unsystematic, vital knowledge by connaturality or congeniality, in which the intellect, in order to bear judgment, consults and listens to the inner melody that the vibrating strings of abiding tendencies make present in the subject" (*Man and the State*).

The words inclination, tendency, congeniality, and connaturality all indicate a primary and intimate relationship between man and nature. By denying this natural relationship, man is left without a starting point. As a consequence, he no longer sees the natural difference between the sexes thereby, in effect, deconstructing its binary quality. He begins his understanding of the sexes on the plane of his own subjectivity. Therefore, sex and gender become whatever he wants them to become.

A United Nations agency has proposed doing away with the words "woman", "feminine", "man" and "masculine", which it now regards as superannuated. It is a supreme irony that feminism, which sought to improve the lives of women, has been marching toward the extinction of the very terms that originally described them. The UN, however, is just one example of cutting human beings off at the roots and attempting to transplant them in an ideological vacuum.

Man is no longer attentive to the "vibrating strings" that are attuned to the natural world. He believes he has gained a new freedom by being emancipated from them. But he is now placed in a moral vacuum and what he believes to be his new freedom is really his doom, for man cannot breathe in a vacuum. Feminists will continue to fight with each other since they have thrown away their common ground. The latest altercation is between feminists who deny that a man can become a woman simply on the basis of an assertion. They call themselves "Trans Exclusionary Radical Feminists". They are regarded as "heretics," by another wing of feminism that includes men who call themselves women and have issued a pamphlet entitled *How to Spot TERF Ideology* to protect themselves against those whom it views as infidels.

D. H. Lawrence has expressed the matter accurately and poetically:

> We are bleeding at the roots, because we are cut off from the earth and sun and stars. Love has become a grinning mockery because, poor blossom, we plucked it from its stem on the Tree of Life and expected it to keep on blooming in our civilized vase on the table.

Life has roots in nature. Nothing grows unless it is properly planted. We transcend nature, but we are nevertheless rooted in it. When we deny our roots, we deny our potential for growth. Without a common ground, the very ground in which we are all rooted, disagreement, demoralization, and division will continue to flourish.

The Shattering of an Image

The distinguished historian Daniel J. Boorstin wrote *The Image: A Guide to Pseudo-events in America* to explain "how we have used our wealth, our literacy, our technology, and our progress, to create a thicket of unreality which stands between us and the facts of life". This unreal world is an image that conceals a reality that, in the view of many, does not have the luster or attractiveness of a beautifully crafted image. As journalist George Will explains:

> Today we see that we are living in a society that increasingly resembles an echo chamber lined with mirrors. Amid the sensory blitzkrieg contemporary life, much that is spoken is merely audio wallpaper.

Once in a while, when death occurs or when something totally unexpected happens, the image is shattered and we are rudely thrown back to reality. Trying to keep reality at a distance is hard work. "Keeping up appearances" requires a great deal of effort. Reality, much to our displeasure, keeps breaking through.

Narcissus fell in love with his image, which he saw reflected in a pool. Echo tried in vain to lure him out of his fixation with himself through love. The word "narcissus" is etymologically related to "narcotic". Narcissus' fate was to allow an illusion to render him numb to his real identity and ultimately destroy it. The image is what we see, even though it is fabricated. The inner person is something we must discover, and that requires patience, effort, and time. The illusion is what we prefer to see even though it is unreal; truth is what we do not want to see, even though it is real. Jack Ruby, who was imprisoned for killing Lee Harvey Oswald, begged his portrait artist to give him a little more hair. Then people could say, "He may have been a murderer, but for a man of his age, he had a good crop of hair." An admiring friend, said, "My, that's a beautiful baby you have there". "Oh, that's nothing," said the mother. "You should see his photograph!" The "photo-op" creates the impression that we are more captivating than we really are in person.

Hollywood has earned the name "Tinsel Town" for its uncompromising dedication to a world of images. Yet, beneath the tinsel, quips Oscar Levant, is 'the real tinsel". Neither glitz, glitter, nor glamor have any depth. Hollywood is a place, according to Groucho Marx, where the bride keeps the flowers and throws away the groom. Its citizens are predictably beautiful, talented, wealthy, well-dressed, and. above all – well-mannered. And then, at the 2022 Academy Awards, something unimaginable, unthinkable, unspeakable, and unprecedented happened. Will Smith rose from his seat, strode to the stage and slapped a defenseless and unprepared Chris Rock across the face while spouting language that is not fit to print. It is one thing for the tabloids to expose the imperfections of movie stars, but it is quite another for a star, himself, to display them for the world to see live.

Had I been a comedy writer and been on stage with Chris Rock, I would have advised him to tell the audience to have sympathy for his assailant because when Will Smith was growing up his favorite comic was Slappy White. Yet, no amount of humor can conceal the enormity of what transpired. Humor may save face, but it cannot erase.

Since this incident took place—"The Slap Heard Round the World"—an enormous amount of attention has been given to Oscar night 2022 which will forever be known as "Slapgate," an invidious association with the most notorious political scandal in American history. Whatever else happened that night fell below the radar. An irremovable scar had marred the face of the Oscar. The evening unequivocally belonged to Will Smith and his egregious violation of Hollywood rules. The sacred image was shattered. Academy Awards night could now be seen as a magnificent masquerade party of people pretending to be something other than what they really are. Hollywood is willing to bare anything but its soul.

"Life is a masquerade full of illusions," wrote the Danish philosopher, Soren Kierkegaard. "Do you not know," he warned, "that there comes a midnight hour when everyone has to throw off his mask? Do you believe that life will always let itself be mocked?" The mask is poor insulation against reality. The truth of one's personality will ultimately be revealed, for good or for ill. The illusions of Hollywood are fodder for the delusions of its fandom.

Will Smith made the obligatory apology. Such apologies are customarily drawn up by lawyers and have the ring of insincerity. But an apology is not a "confession," in the true sense of that term. To confess one's sins to a priest requires setting aside any image of oneself and laying bare one's soul. A person cannot bring a lawyer with him into the confessional box and ask for a lighter penance. We are all stained by Original Sin. This simple fact exposes the futility of images. The confession is a meeting between man and God in which pretensions are strictly forbidden. It is a moment of truth. But also of reconciliation.

Christ made it only too clear that the pretentious Pharisees were not good role models. He requires us to be true to ourselves, to know that we are fallen creatures and in need of His grace. Catholicism has nothing in common with a masquerade party.

WHO ARE THE BARBARIANS OF TODAY?

Harsha Walia, a month after she called for Catholic churches to be burned "down", resigned from her post as executive director of a Canadian civil rights group after a public outcry. She sparked an online fury in calling for violence against Catholic churches stating, "Burn it all down". Nonetheless, her approval of violence was not without support from the legal profession.

Rebel News founder Ezra Levant, in a *FOX News* interview hosted by Tucker Carlson, stated that the multitude of arson attacks on churches in Canada is Canada's "Black Lives Matter"

movement and called out the nation's top leaders for their near silence regarding the burnings. Carlson has said that "all of a sudden Canada looks a lot like the Soviet Union."

It is significant that people who profess to support human rights today can think along the lines of barbarians. George Will wrote *Statecraft as Soulcraft* (1983) in response to what he termed the "slow-motion barbarization" that he perceived in American politics. There are barbarians operating among us who are arrayed in sheep's clothing and supposedly represent honorable interests.

The word 'barbarian' originated in ancient Greece. The barbarian (*bàrbaros*) was someone who spoke in a non-Greek language which was unintelligible to the Greek ear. The term was specifically directed to Persians, Egyptians, Medes and Phoenicians. It was as though these so-called barbarians were simply uttering "bar-bar-bar". Consequently, the barbarians were incoherent "babblers". Late in the Roman Empire, the term applied to those who lacked Greek or Roman traditions, specifically to Goths, Huns, Vandals, and Saxons.

In the year 410 A.D., the barbarians sacked Rome. St. Augustine wrote his monumental *De Civitate Dei* (*The City of God*) to defend Christianity from the charge that it was responsible for the calamity.

> Here, then is this Roman republic, 'which has changed little by little from the fair and virtuous city it was, and has become utterly wicked and dissolute. It is not I who am the first to say this, but their own authors, from whom we learned it . . . and who wrote it long before the coming of Christ. You see how [the Romans] were swept away as by a torrent; and how depraved by luxury and avarice the youth were (Book II, Ch. 19).

We could use another Augustine to answer the false claim that Canadian Catholics are today's real barbarians.

We have now come to think of barbarians as uncivilized, uncouth, and lacking appreciation for anything outside of their own insular frame of reference. In hindsight, according to the modern usage of the term, the real barbarian of antiquity was the ancient Greek or Roman since he shut himself off from a broader awareness of things. The modern barbarian is one who regards anything outside of his own frame of reference as incoherent and consequently worthless. He is like the British soldiers during the India rebellion who defaced the Taj Mahal, or Oliver Cromwell who went on a rampage destroying numerous Catholic churches.

Here we may ask the questions, "Who is the barbarian of today?" "Does the word apply to the Catholic whose doctrine is regarded by many as unintelligible, or to those who do not make the effort to understand the richness of Catholic teaching?" The word Catholic, meaning "universal," would suggest that the true Catholic is interested in a wide variety of things. By the same token, the pro-life person, often denigrated as extremely narrow, is interested in defending the life of all human beings.

Alistair MacIntyre, in his book, *After Virtue*, contends that we are now in the same situation as the ancient Greeks and Romans. With regard to moral discourse, the new barbarians are those who neither speak nor understand the language of the moral tradition that has shaped the relatively humanitarian world we call Western civilization. They regard arguments put forward to defend traditional marriage, the dignity of life, the natural law, and even God's existence as unintelligible. The late Rev. Richard John Neuhaus has added the statement that "Once anyone steps outside this [Western] tradition, then that person is considered a barbarian." C. S. Lewis offered an antidote to the cultural blindness that forms the mind of the barbarian when he advised people "to keep the clean sea breeze of the centuries blowing through our minds . . . by reading good books."

Hilaire Belloc (1870-1953), fittingly known as "Old Thunder," dedicated a chapter called "The Barbarians" in his 1912 book, *This That and the Other*. He speaks about how we sit by and watch the barbarian and find his antics amusing. To our discredit, we tolerate that which we should oppose. He writes:

> We are ticked by his irreverence, his comic inversion of our old certitudes and our fixed creeds refreshes us: we laugh. But as we laugh we are watched by large and awful faces from beyond: and on these faces there is no smile.

In reading Belloc the spectacle of marches that promote the homosexual life-style come to mind. Their participants live off the capital derived from the very tradition they denounce. But they have no real contribution to make for a replacement. They are a spectacle cut off from both the past and the future. They demand attention but have nothing positive to offer.

Belloc, however, is more concerned about the factors that create a place for the barbarians. He recognizes that society is an organism and as such, it must be able to reject elements that are inimical to it. Therefore, he writes, "Whoever would restore any society which menaces to fall, must busy himself about the inward nature of that society much more than about its external dangers or the merely mechanical and numerical factors or peril to be discovered within it."

Applying Belloc's thinking to the present day world, a weakened society that cannot protect itself against harmful alien elements is like an organism with AIDS whose immune system is too enfeebled to reject harmful substances that attack it. The society that goes out of its way to invite harmful elements into its system is like a society afflicted with AIDS. Belloc's comments, though penned in 1912, are valid for all times.

In returning to the question, "Who are the barbarians?" the answer devolves upon those who have cut themselves off from tradition and regard its contribution to religion, education, and morality as unintelligible. By contrast, the educated person, for whom Plato, Aristotle, Aquinas, Milton, Shakespeare, Bach, Beethoven, Newton, and Einstein are always relevant, is open to the great lessons of history. He is the person who does not allow himself to be limited either by time or space. Thomas Sowell has put the matter in a nutshell:

> Each new generation is in effect an invasion of civilization by little barbarians, who must be civilized before it is too late.

BIGOTRY

When I was very young and growing up in an Italian family, I thought the word "bigotry" referred to an unusually large tree.** My grandfather would say, "Hey, dat's a biga tree". But now that I am much older and have transferred my trust from my paternal grandfather to the mass media, I realize that bigotry is being a Christian who stands up for his principles and opposes sin — at least that is what Sarah Spain is telling us on a popular sports show, *Around the Horn*.

The new usage of the word bigotry is really a libelous attack against five Tampa Bay baseball players who declined wearing

a pride flag on their uniforms. Sarah Spain stated, on air, that the players who do not wear a pride flag are bigoted and are using an adulterated religion to justify their position. The players said nothing about anyone and they were given the option not to wear the pride emblems. Yet, they were vilified.

Not everyone agreed with Ms. Spain's accusations. Sport's writer, Clay Travis, for example, felt that her comments had no place on a sports program: "Imagine turning on sports and getting this loony left wing insanity on your TV. Embarrassing." The sports-minded fan is not interested in viewing a battle between the "bigots" and the "loonies". Matt Walsh, a writer for the Daily Wire added this blistering comment: "Now they're trying to cancel people for not wearing a gay pride patch, this is always the trajectory for the Left. First they demand tolerance, then acceptance, then celebration, then participation. Learn to say no to these people or it will never end." The Tampa Bay "five" deserve praise. Their personal choice does not warrant criticism. Former NFL star, Benjamin Watson put things in the proper perspective in saying that "It is imperative that sports teams never force employees to participate in messaging and displays outside of sport specific obligations. . . . I applaud these men for standing in love and truth and for supporting their convictions."

In certain political circles, Sarah Spain's harangue would qualify for "hate speech". But people in the media are treated differently in accordance with their political views. Legendary pitcher Curt Schilling, holds the record for the best winning percentage in post season play with 11 wins and only 2 losses. His weekly radio show raised $100,000 a year for amyotrophic lateral sclerosis (Lou Gehrig's disease). His stature as a major league baseball player and philanthropist, however, was not as important to ESPN as political correctness. He was fired because he made the unforgivable "mistake" of stating that the men's room is for men and the women's room is for women.

The network's executive statement reads as follows: "ESPN is an inclusive company and Curt Schilling has been advised that this conduct was unacceptable and his employment with ESPN has been terminated." He was excluded by a policy that demands inclusivity. It is not easy these days to navigate in a culture of contradictions.

In an atmosphere of totalitarianism in which everyone is compelled to think and act in the same way, Christianity must be kept under wraps or else it is attacked. Christianity's teaching simply does not fit in to a culture that has lost its moral sense. The love that is the essence of Christianity is inseparable from disapproving sins that are injurious to the soul. Those who would want to live by sin cannot tolerate their critics, even when their criticism is tacit. They reach for the nearest weapon on the table, "bigotry," if not "racism" or "sexism," and aim it at their alleged oppressors. Psychologists call this "projection". Christ was executed because people could not accept the higher standard of life that He was preaching. They preferred Barabbas, the reprobate. And yet, in the aftermath of the crucifixion His death liberated an endless number of souls who thirsted for His message.

One of the great attractions of sports is that it presents to both the participant and the spectator a refuge from the disorderliness of the world. Umpires preside over the game of baseball to ensure that its rules are observed. The game cannot be played without strict compliance to these rules. The strike zone and the foul poles define its parameters. Balls and strikes, safe and out, win and lose are the outcomes of each play. The rules of baseball present a paragon of order. A runner must get to first base before he is eligible to get to second. The batting order is a model of fairness. Each player, no matter his rank, status, color, or creed, must wait for his turn at bat. We need an antidote to the chaos of life. Sports, at least to a certain extent, provides this. Sarah Spain's anti-Christian accusations have no business on a sports show. Nor do they have any justification under any circumstances. The viewer, listening to her rant, will inevitably ask himself the question, "Who is the bigot?"

In retrospect, I think that my grandfather's Italianization of the word "bigotry" was closer to the truth than the version we get on a particular sport's program. At any rate, it has the glorious merit of being amusing and innocuous.

A Bouquet of Blunders

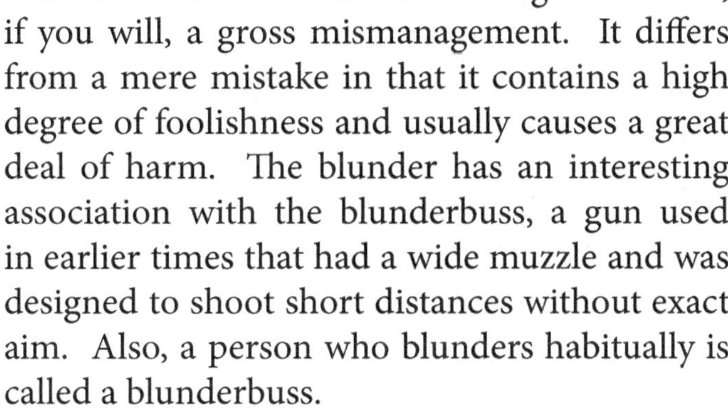

A **bouquet of flowers is more presentable than a bouquet of blunders.** Nonetheless, looking over the contemporary moral landscape, it is the blunders that are flourishing and not the flowers. A blunder is a big mistake or, if you will, a gross mismanagement. It differs from a mere mistake in that it contains a high degree of foolishness and usually causes a great deal of harm. The blunder has an interesting association with the blunderbuss, a gun used in earlier times that had a wide muzzle and was designed to shoot short distances without exact aim. Also, a person who blunders habitually is called a blunderbuss.

My dozen blunders, outlined below, help to explain the moral confusion that prevails in present day society.

1) **Love is an emotion.** Love, properly understood, is the will to promote the good of the other. The beloved is a necessary concomitant to the lover. The lover may or may not feel emotion when he loves, but it is the will to serve the good of the other that is primary. The emotion is secondary. Whereas the emotion may be delightful, love is often difficult. We have a duty to love, but not to enjoy the emotion. Love is both realistic as well as altruistic.

2) **Sex is an amusement.** According to the nature of things, sex is ordinated to life. Contraception, sterilization, and abortion sever the intrinsic connection that naturally exists between sex and procreation. Sex is fundamentally pro-creational rather than recreational. Like love, sex is related to the other. Amusement is related to the self. Sex is also naturally ordinated to love and marriage. To reduce sex to amusement is to trivialize a profound and meaningful gift.

3) **Marriage is a convention.** If marriage were merely a convention any arrangement between people could be called a marriage. Therefore, marriage would become meaningless. History has shown, however, that the marriage between a man and a woman bound together in a committed and unselfish love has been not only a great blessing to society, but has served as its fundamental basis. No other arrangement is so naturally suited to inspire love and responsibility toward children.

4) **Religion is an invention.** Religion must be relatable to God. Therefore, it cannot be subjective. The more people try to make religion their own, the less they make it a religion. The two primary purposes of religion is to worship God and become more God-like by adopting the virtues of faith, hope, and charity. Religion makes moral demands on us. In this sense religion afflicts the comfortable in addition to comforting the afflicted.

5) **The natural law is a construct.** Nature is stubbornly objective. It precedes society or any social construct. In this sense it is original. It is also universal. Scientists who study nature understand this and therefore can work together as a fraternity. Nature is also a principle of growth. Human nature applies to all human beings. Because it is a principle of growth, it gives us a sense of where we are going and what we must do in order to fulfill ourselves. This is not something that anyone has invented.

6) **Abortion is a choice.** Abortion is more than a choice since it produces a train of consequences. Many of these con-

sequences, affecting the aborting woman, marriage, the family, and society in general, are deleterious and would not be chosen if they were known. To make a choice while being blind to its consequences is more like a guess than an enlightened choice. Moreover, the so called "choice" is at variance with the developing child in the womb that, according to its natural impulses, is persistently choosing life.

7) **Euthanasia is death with dignity.** Dignity is an intrinsic quality that is irremovable. Human beings have an inalienable dignity that cannot be lost. To say that a person can be put to death with dignity is to suggest that he would forfeit dignity if he were to remain alive. If there is no dignity in a particular person who is alive, it is difficult to understand how that person could gain dignity by being put to death.

8) **A human being is an autonomous individual.** All human beings are finite, mortal, and defectible. They are subject to chance, violence, ageing, and death. It is the height of ignorance to claim that anyone can be or achieve autonomy. In addition, human beings need other human beings. They live by love and thrive through cooperation. Autonomy is a myth that lacks all plausibility.

9) **Education is adaptation to the times.** The most important feature of education is to teach a person how to be a more complete human being. Personal excellence is the fundamental objective of education. As a secondary feature, it prepares a person for his role in society. But a person is ill-suited for that role if he has not been prepared as an authentic, moral human being.

10) **The meaning of life is subjective.** Human beings belong to a society, a commonwealth in which each individual has a contribution to make so that that society can prosper and flourish. Each person has his own subjectivity in the sense that he is unique. Nonetheless, the ultimate value of that uniqueness is

realized in how a person is able to bring his uniqueness to bear for the common good.

11) **Gender is fluid.** All societies throughout human history have recognized the binary quality of persons as male or female. As it is in the case of animals, this binary quality is essential for reproduction. Maleness or femaleness is marked in our genes. Its basis is natural and biological. The current fashion to invent a superfluity of genders has no realistic basis.

12) **God is a fiction.** The current trend toward atheism fails to come to terms with the designs of nature as well as the designs of the cosmos. The world could not have emerged from nothingness and no finite being could have created the sun, the moon, and the stars. Also, there must be a God to account for our belief in love, our thirst for justice and our desire for eternal life.

A common denominator for these twelve blunders is a rejection of God and a retreat into the solitary self.

75

A Performance of the Farce
Pieter Balten (Flemish. c. 1527 - 1584)

PART TWO

THE CALM AFTER THE STORM

How Should I Begin?

In every enterprise it is better to begin at the beginning. This is not a guaranteed formula for success, but it does offer the best chance for achieving success.

How should I begin the day: with coffee, turning on the radio, opening the newspaper? Or with a prayer that begins with making the sign of the cross? The beginning sets the tone and places us on the right track. It opens vistas in which everything is in the correct order. The day may get off the track, as days often do, but this was not for failing to begin where it should begin.

"The beginning is the most important part of the work," wrote Plato. Consider the first four notes that open Beethoven's Fifth Symphony and how important they were to everything that flowed from them. "A small mistake in the beginning," wrote Ar-

istotle, "is a big one in the end." The beginning sets the course. Let us begin a meal with a prayer. That way a five course meal becomes a six course meal.

When it comes to participating in a sporting event, I should begin with confidence. I may eventually lose, but I have little chance of winning if I approach the event with losing firmly entrenched in my mind. In business, a man begins with advertising. He must let people know what he has for sale. Advertising is prudent but offers no guarantee of sales. A politician should be honest at the outset and try to retain that virtue throughout his life in politics. Yet we all know how easily honesty can give way to deceitfulness. Let us begin marriage with love and pray that it perseveres, that it does not bend under pressure, but "looks on tempests and is never shaken" (Shakespeare, *Sonnet 116*). Would that all marriages that commence with love could maintain that worthy virtue.

The scientist, facing a broad and mysterious world, should begin with an open mind. He does not want to introduce private preferences or political assumptions into his equations. Nonetheless, this attitude is not easy to maintain. In theology, where we encounter truths that transcend our comprehension, we begin with faith. Once again, this noble and necessary virtue often gives way to criticism, doubt, and rejection. Scoring five runs in the first inning gets us off to a good start, but by no means does it assure victory.

Philosophy must begin with wonder if it is to have any chance of attaining wisdom. Throughout history various thinkers, calling themselves philosophers, began with a desire to be novel, or an attempt to achieve power, fortune, or fame. The true philosopher begins with discernible effects and begins a slow journey toward the wondrous causes that produced them which often lie beyond his ken. He advances with humility and must never bargain away his initial and childlike sense of wonder.

I want to expand a little on where one should begin the art of teaching philosophy. Students have strongly held positions, whether or not these positions are justified. An inevitable tension exists between teacher and student. How should I begin a philosophy course so as to minimize conflict and maximize learning? I begin with but a single ally – reason. I may say to my students the following:

We are rational beings, though we often fail to honor this universal possession that marks our nature as members of the human family. Consider how extensively you employed reason in getting here today. Without the use of reason, you could not begin to maneuver through this labyrinth of life. None of you, I trust, would prefer to be insane. Without the light of reason, we are entirely helpless. Therefore, let us call upon reason to guide us through this course, hoping to enlighten and not offend, to inspire and not stimulate revolt. We are united together by the firm chord of reason. Does anyone here have any rational objections to the use of reason?

And what is often the result? Emotion, prejudice, and convenience have a way of usurping the throne of reason and installing themselves in its place. Yet this is no reason to despair. One cannot do anything better than placing his trust in reason at the starting gate.

We turn to the question, "How did God Begin"? "In the beginning was the Word," St. John tells us. Christ, as the Word made Flesh, often used parables about seeds and sowing. He even referred to Himself as a "seed". In his compendious book, *Life of Christ*, Archbishop Fulton J. Sheen states that "The Word

is the seed". In one of Christ's parables, he compares His Mission to a seed falling on different kinds of earth in order to explain the different responses that souls make to His inviting grace.

> Behold, the sower went forth to sow; and as he sowed, some seeds fell by the wayside, and the birds came and devoured them; some fell upon stony places, where they had not much earth; and forthwith they sprung up, because they had no deepness of earth: and when the sun was up, they were scorched; and because they had no root, they withered away. And some fell among thorns; and the thorns sprung up, and choked them: but others fell into good ground, and brought forth fruit, some a hundredfold, some sixtyfold, some thirtyfold (Matt. 13:1-9; 18-23).

Christ came not in the raiment of a king but in the role of a sower.

If Christ can sometimes fail in his attempt to inspire souls in accepting His Word, why should we be discouraged when we sometimes fail in our various enterprises? The teacher plants  seeds and hopes that they will germinate in the minds and hearts of his students. He should not abandon the value of his beginning simply because he has experienced momentary setbacks. We begin at the beginning and pray for perseverance. We walk in the footsteps of Christ and are prepared to accept the trips and tumbles that are inevitable along the way.

Is Truth Objective?

The question concerning the objectivity of truth is deceptive. It presupposes that truth might not be objective. But truth and objectivity are inseparable. From a philosophical perspective, the question is rather odd, like asking whether a lion is an animal. The assertion that a lion is an animal at the same time tells a truth about the lion and is never questioned. No one ever raises the question. It would never appear in a zoology text. Yet, this curious question concerning the objectivity of truth is standard fare for philosophy text books.

Perhaps the best and most convincing way to answer the problem is to approach it from the rear. Everyone knows that there is such a thing as a lie. In a text book on ethics, the question

"Is there such a thing as a lie," never appears. We are certain that there are lies only because they are deviations from truth. During court proceedings a witness swears to tell "the truth, the whole truth and nothing but the truth". Perjury, which is telling a lie under oath, is a serious violation of the law and is punishable. A lie, therefore, is a deliberate falsification of the truth. If there are no truths, there cannot be any lies. If there are no animals, there cannot be any lions. When a judge makes a decision based on objective evidence, he renders a "verdict," a most revealing word since it is derived from two Latin words – *verum* and *dicere*, meaning "to tell the truth". The objectivity of truth is the basis of law. There could be no legal system, justice, or jurisprudence without a clear recognition of the objectivity of truth.

Similarly, the search for truth is the guiding principle of science and is the objective reality that unifies all scientists. It is also the basis of medicine. A doctor wants to discover what is wrong with his patient. He is not satisfied until he uncovers the truth. Without truth all of reality would crumble into in indecipherable mishmash, an unintelligible chaos. History, it should be plain to everyone, is the great defender of truth. Sometimes truth is difficult to find. When certain individuals claim they have discovered some nugget of truth, they are often regarded with suspicion or, as in the cases of such stalwarts as Columbus, Pasteur, Kepler, and others, become objects of ridicule.

We also recognize the objectivity of truth when it is replaced to subserve a political ideology. The renowned philosopher, Dietrich von Hildebrand, cites an example of politics replacing philosophy in a chapter he calls, "The Dethronement of Truth" from his book, *The New Tower of Babel*. He quotes Hans Schemm, the Bavarian minister of education who, in 1933, solemnly declared before an assemblage of university professors the following:

From this day on, you will no longer have to examine whether something is true or not, but exclusively whether or not it corresponds to the Nazi ideology.

Commenting on this outrageous displacement of truth to make room for a Nazi ideology, von Hildebrand, made the remark that:

Conformity to the feelings of the Nordic race or of
the German people replaced every objective standard
of truth, goodness, beauty, and right.

Just as Nazism fed people with lies, Communism in Russia did the same. Nobel Prize winter, Alexander Solzhenitsyn famously responded to this travesty by stating, "One word of truth outweighs the world."

Truth can be inconvenient for those who are in power. They may deny the objective reality of truth because its gets in the way of their nefarious plans. Truth is often denied when it is too painful to bear. The sudden death of a loved one, or the unexpected bad news from a doctor may initially be denied. Psychiatrist Elisabeth Kübler-Ross made an

important contribution to her field in reporting the "five stages of grief" that dying patients experience as they pass through denial, anger, bargaining, and depression, before reaching acceptance.

Pope St. John Paul II's encyclical, *Veritatis Splendor,* is essentially an affirmation of the objectivity of truth. The former pontiff builds upon Christ's statement that "You will know the truth, and the truth will make you free" (John 8: 32). But the encyclical is also philosophical. He speaks of "the crisis of truth" that exists in the world. This crisis is exemplified by people exchanging the objectivity of truth for the subjectivity of personal convenience. As the title indicates, truth has a certain light (splendor) that shines to make it eminently recognizable. But in addition to being knowable, living with truth is immensely beneficial to everyone. Pope St. John Paul states:

Thus, in every sphere of personal, family, social and

political life, morality — founded upon truth and open in truth to authentic freedom — renders a primordial, indispensable and immensely valuable service not only for the individual person and his growth in the good, but also for society and its genuine development.

The truth may not be as difficult to recognize as it is to put into practice. In this regard, truth is regarded as inconvenient,  frustrating, or impractical. Therefore, many people are tempted to deny something they really know. We speak the lie, but hide from the truth. When Cain said, "Am I my brother's keeper," he was aware of the lie he put forward to the one who knew the truth of what happened. We are subjects. As a result, we are tempted to interpret things, not realistically, but to our advantage, that is, subjectively. The truth, however, has a way of catching up with us. St. Thomas Aquinas put the matter quite simply when he wrote,

> The human intellect is measured by things so that man's thought is not true on its own account but is called true in virtue of its conformity with things (*Summa Theologica* 19, 8, ad 2).

It should be clear that truth is objective. What has happened in the modern world is that psychology has overtaken philosophy and, for psychological reasons, the objectivity of truth is questioned, denied, found too painful, or dismissed. It is precisely because philosophy is connected with reality, that it cannot be replaced either by psychology, politics, or any ideology that is rooted in subjective advantage.

Why Are There Stairs?

William J. Bennett, former Secretary of Education, under President Reagan, came to the conclusion during his tenure in office that most of education

consists in restating the obvious. I shall begin this essay with the question, "Why Are There Stairs"? This should not be a difficult question to answer, though I can imagine that there are competing answers. Stairs exist so that we can get to a higher level. We speak of a "flight of stairs," suggesting that they rise, akin to the way an airplane takes flight. Now it is true that a staircase serves a twofold purpose: descending as well as ascending. But the primary purpose of stairs is to ascend. We speak of elevators, not de-elevators, escalators, not de-escalators, and, in the British vernacular, lifts, not drops. The upward trajectory of stairs is further emphasized by expressions such as "Let's build a stairway to the stars," or a "stairway to heaven". It is also true that we can fall down the stairs, but that is not the purpose of stairs.

The notion of using stairs as a means of moving to a higher level symbolizes life. In this regard, Jacob's dream "in which he saw a stairway on earth, with its top reaching heaven" (Genesis 28:12), is richly symbolic. We all rise in the morning. Some hope to climb the corporate ladder, while others pray that they may come closer to God. There are times when we need to have our spirits uplifted. We are advised to "cheer up" and to "keep our chin up". "Up" seems to be where we want to go. Mountaineers cannot resist climbing mountains to get to the top. If there is a single word that epitomizes the legacy of ancient Greece, it is "aspiration," the natural desire to attain something higher.

"Stairs" is analogous with freedom. The purpose of freedom of choice is to use that freedom wisely so that we can attain freedom of fulfillment. Jacques Maritain has referred to this kind of freedom as "freedom of autonomy". To remain on the level of freedom of choice is to remain on the ground floor and not to ascend to the penthouse. Freedom of fulfillment is on a higher level than freedom of choice. How do we get to this higher level? We use reason, which is our veritable staircase. We use reason to put our life in order. Acquaintance, friendship, love, and willingness to make a commitment, in that order, seem to be required before marriage. To employ a dubious pun, we should not stare at the steps, but step on the stairs. Life is an upward journey. Sloth is the deadly sin that keeps us at ground level.

Some time ago, in an attempt to assess the aftermath of sexual permissiveness on the campus of a major North American university, I spoke with the director of the school's Birth Control and Sex Information Centre. By way of summarizing what she had informed me, I said to her, "You have observed a tidal wave of premarital sex, a rash of unwanted pregnancies, a high number of abortions together with their train of complications, an epidemic of sexually transmitted diseases, a widespread disruption of studying in the dorms, an increasing disrespect for women, and an intolerance toward the minority of students who are opposed to premarital sexual experimentation". I then asked her if there was anything positive on the other side of the ledger that might counterbalance this plague of misfortunes.

She hesitated for a moment. Without taking her eyes away from me, she responded in a studied tone of voice, "Yes, the freedom!" On that note, our conversation ended. There would be no development in our conversation. There would be no staircase to permit moving to a higher level of freedom. She excused herself and hurried off to her next appointment. I sensed that she was not altogether happy with her single word defense.

It is a sad commentary on present day society that so many people, students especially, believe that any expression of freedom of choice is self-justifying. To exclude freedom of fulfillment from the equation, however, is to deny the validity of morality. Such a denial would inevitably lead to chaos. Surely education and chaos are sworn enemies. The aim of education is to help people put their lives in order so that their lives have meaning. Contemporary film director, Werner Herzog has said that "Civilization is like a thin layer of ice upon a deep ocean of chaos and darkness". All that is need for chaos to bob to the surface is for freedom of fulfillment to be severed from freedom of choice.

In his encyclical, *Veritatis Splendor*, Pope St. John Paul II unites the two freedoms when he states that "Acting is morally good when the choices of freedom are in conformity with man's true good and thus express the voluntary ordering of the person towards his ultimate end." Moving in the direction of one's end is a voluntary activity. This voluntary activity, however, exists not for itself, but for a higher end.

My colleague at the university did not seem to recognize the essential importance of freedom of fulfillment. I became an antagonist because I did not share her truncated philosophy. She was loyal to students who were not loyal to themselves. Torn between the risk of offending them and not providing any direction, she chose the latter.

I think that William Bennett, as an educator, would classify the innate and unbreakable relationship between freedom of choice and freedom of fulfillment as fairly obvious. Unhappily, what seems obvious these days has become mysterious.

Geometry and Justice

Geometry teaches us more than geometry. It supplies us with lessons that are actually indispensable for morality. A triangle is a three-sided two dimensional figure whose interior angles add up to 180 degrees. That is the definition of a triangle. An equilateral triangle has three equal sides, an isosceles triangle has two equal sides, and a scalene triangle has no equal sides. They are different, but they all conform to the definition of a triangle. No geometer would disagree. Engineering would not be possible if engineers began treating triangles as squares and squares as triangles. In this regard, there is peaceful conformity between all triangles and their unifying definition.

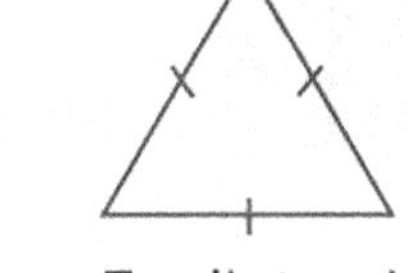

Equilateral
All three sides are equal

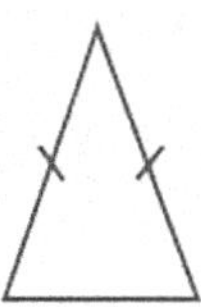

Isosceles
Two sides are equal

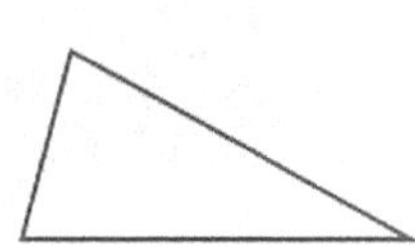

Scalene
No sides are equal

A human being is a rational creature endowed by God with unalienable dignity. It does not matter whether a human being is white, black, or brown, Christian, Jew, or Muslim. All these types correspond to the definition of a human being. It would be wrong to deny humanity to any of these types. Geometry, then, gives us a fundamental model of justice. If someone conforms to the definition of a human being, then, he is a human being. Justice has a kind of geometric quality in that it equalizes the particular with the universal, just as a scalene triangle, despite its three unequal sides, is still a triangle.

A square has four sides. Therefore, it does not qualify as being a triangle. If a medical doctor is not interested in health, he cannot claim to be a medical doctor. Here, there is an unbridgeable discrepancy between what he does and what he claims to be. Likewise, if the home plate umpire is not concerned about the strike zone, he is not an umpire. And if a lawyer rejects justice, he disqualifies himself from being a lawyer.

UMPIRE IN EDEN

"STRIKE ONE!
YOU'RE OUT!"

Racism, which is universally deplored, is a species of prejudice. A person is said to be prejudicial when he negatively evaluates a person not in relation to that person but in relation to a group or class of which he is a member. Such an act is decidedly unfair. Therefore, prejudice is a species of injustice. Racism and prejudice are both examples of injustice.

In America's fight against racism, strangely enough, it ignores prejudices against Catholics. But one wonders if the fight against racism is pure if it is separated from a more general fight against all forms of prejudice. We would expect that lawyers, who commit themselves to defending justice, would be in the trenches fighting against all forms of injustice, including prejudice against Catholics. Unfortunately, this is not the case. In fact, in some circles, prejudice against Catholics is seen as politically acceptable and even career-advancing.

In late 2018, while evaluating the nomination of Brian Buescher to serve as a district judge in Nebraska, Kamala Harris posed a series of questions insinuating that his involvement in the Knights of Columbus disqualified him from serving on the bench (*National Review*, Alexandra Desanctis, Aug, 11, 2020 "Kamala Harris' Anti-Catholic Bigotry"). She asked him if he were "aware that the Knights of Columbus opposed marriage equality when [he] joined the organization" and whether he had "ever, in any way, assisted with or contributed to advocacy against women's reproductive rights."

Following Harris, Democratic senator from Hawaii, Mazie Hirono, went a bit further, asking Buescher whether he intended to "end [his] membership with this organization to avoid any appearance of bias" — in other words, intimating that she would withhold her vote at least until he had left the Knights of Columbus. At the behest of Nebraska senator, Ben Sasse, Buescher was eventually confirmed. It is important to note that the Senate later voted unanimously to reaffirm the constitutional clause forbidding religious tests for public officeholders. But the fact remains that Harris was guilty of reprehensible anti-Catholic bigotry, and there's no reason to believe her views have changed. She is now Joe Biden's Vice-presidential running mate.

It is worth pointing out that the United States Supreme Court includes five Catholics. And it is clear from recent decisions that they do not think alike or vote in the same way. The notion that a Catholic is unfit to be a judge simply because he is a Catholic is a clear instance of injustice as well as prejudice. The more relevant question is whether a lawyer can call herself a lawyer if she is an enemy of justice? Newt Gingrich, former Speaker of the House has stated on Fox News that:

> The consequences of Harris' openly anti-Catholic bias will be felt as other anti-Catholics draw encouragement from her bigotry to increase the activism and intensity of their assaults on Catholic institutions and Catholic personalities.

If a Catholic is a true Catholic, then he affirms that justice is not only a virtue, but a cardinal virtue along with prudence, fortitude, and wisdom. A true Catholic, then, precisely because he is Catholic, has a credential for being a judge. His appointment to the bench should be welcomed, not disqualified. Here we have, in the examples of Harris and Hirono, two individuals who presume to be defenders of justice but are really its antagonists. Their conduct should ignite a national outrage. Nevertheless, in certain instances, justice continues to take a back seat to political correctness.

The fight against racism should be based on a fight against all forms of injustice. It remains forever that all triangles—equilateral, isosceles and scalene — are all equally triangles. It also remains forever that all human beings are human beings, notwithstanding their color, creed, or affiliation. If America fights injustice selectively, it has not begun the fight.

JOHN PAUL II

THE THEOLOGY OF THE BODY

HUMAN LOVE IN THE DIVINE PLAN

THE THEOLOGY OF THE BODY REVISITED

n December, 1987, a group of distinguished Christian leaders, mostly evangelical, formed The Council on Biblical Manhood and Womanhood. An important factor that led to its formation was what these leaders perceived as "the widespread uncertainty and confusion in our culture regarding the complementary differences between masculinity and femininity". The group's first meeting took place in Danvers, Massachusetts and led to the production of a collection of 31 essays, appropriately called *The Danvers Statement.* Its final form was published the following year.

The CBMW expressed the hope that "the noble Biblical vision of sexual complementarity may yet win the mind and heart of Christ's church". To this end, the group was committed "to study and set forth the Biblical view of the relationship between men and women, especially in the home and in the church". In addition, its members pledged "to encourage the confidence of lay people to study and understand for themselves the teaching of Scripture, especially on the issue of the relationships between men and women". Denial of the fundamental principles concerning the Biblical views of the complementary relationship between men and women, according to the 30 members of the group, "will lead to increasingly destructive consequences in our families, our churches, and the culture at large". The group was indeed prescient.

The Christian leaders of the CBMW group, despite the timeliness of their publication, had no idea of the extent to which the notion of the relationship between men and women would deteriorate, far beyond the level of "uncertainty and confusion" that is currently on display in 2022. Transition from one sex to another, even for children, is now mainstream and its proponents do not tolerate any discussion on the matter. Those who support the Biblical vision of the sexes are out on the defensive. In some instances, they have lost their jobs.

A simple example of the mainstream character of transgenderism provides an accurate snapshot of how it has been granted power and prestige. A MasterCard commercial portrays a transgendered person who is elated that his new name now appears on his credit card. "At last," he happily exclaims, "my card shows the name I have chosen". Transgendered people have a freedom of choice that is not readily available to those who populate the world of the non-transgendered. MasterCard, not Scripture, is now in charge!

A few years prior to the Danvers Statement, in September of 1979, Pope St. John Paul II launched his *Theology of the Body*. The first of four sections of this monumental work consists of twenty-three catechises, drawing on the theme found in a phrase from Christ's dispute with the Pharisees concerning the impermissibility of divorce: "Have you not read that He who made them from the beginning made them male and female?" (Matthew 19.4). John Paul expands on this theme in a way that is both scholarly and eminently readable.

The 130 texts in John Paul's *Theology of the Body* concluded in November, 1984. George Weigel, author of *Witness to Hope*, the authoritative biography of the pope, has stated that if this work receives the attention it deserves, it "may prove to be the decisive moment in exorcising the Manichaean demon and its depreciation of human sexuality from Catholic moral theology". Human sexuality is not, in itself, shameful; it is God-given. Few theologians have taken the distinctiveness and relationship between the sexes as seriously as Pope St. John Paul II has. In the opinion of Weigel, the *Theology of the Body* is "a kind of time bomb set to go off, with dramatic consequences sometime in the third millennium of the church". It is, of course, still early in the millennium, though one might hear the faint sound of ticking.

While John Paul II affirms the Biblical vision of the sexes, he is careful to include a well thought out anthropological realism that answers the question, "What is man?" In this case, theology and philosophy are perfectly in tune with each other. A human being is made to love and does not fulfill his humanity when he does not love. For John Paul, the "complete and definitive creation of 'man' occurs only when God created Eve. Men and women are made in the image of God not only intellectually and emotionally, but above all "through the communion of persons which man and woman form right from the beginning . . . Man becomes the image of God . . . in the moment of communion".

The Danvers Statement and Pope St. John Paul II's *Theology of the Body* are in perfect agreement mutual agreement. Moreover, they give added credibility to each other. They have reached a kind of ecumenical consensus. Together they make for timely reading if one wants to understand the relationship between men and women on a level other than sound-bites and mass media propaganda. The complementarity between the sexes is critical for marriage and the family to fulfill their obligations. There is hardly anything more important in today's confused world than getting right what is most essential. Although the now sainted John Paul II completed his *Theology of the Body* some twenty-eight years ago, it has not aged and remains timely reading. It is worth revisiting.

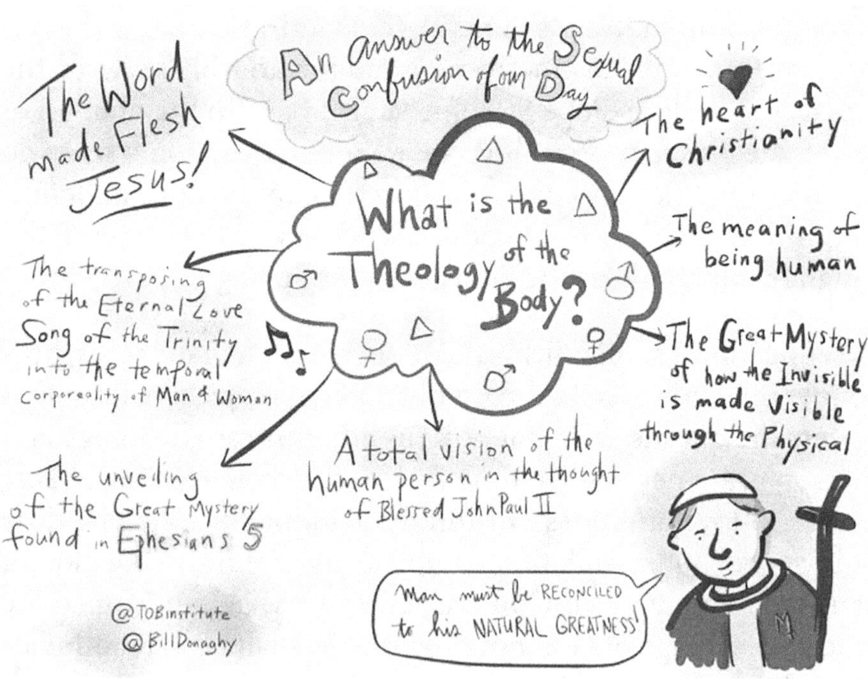

The Problem in Recognizing Our Sins

We build skyscrapers, split the atom, design computers, and send men to the moon, but the most difficult and most important task remains undone, namely acknowledging our personal sins. Pride, the most deceptive of the Seven Deadly Sins, creates the illusion that we are better than we are and therefore renders critical self-examination unnecessary. "I don't want criticism," insisted Mussolini, "I want applause".

How can those who favor abortion acknowledge its iniquity? Abortion is the deliberate killing of an innocent human being. It is robbing that human being of ever knowing love, liberty, or life. It is an evil of such enormity that it is too painful to acknowledge and much easier to repress. The self-justification of an evil must close itself off from self-realization. As a consequence, the person who represses his complicity in evil acts must war against anyone who seeks to liberate him from his delusions. Nothing is more horrifying to a person than the sudden realization of his repressed iniquities.

The story of King David offers us the first of four examples concerning individuals who could not acknowledge their sins, but through the grace of God and the help of others, experienced an epiphany which led to their conversions and to a far better life. David, despite his many wives and concubines, lusted after Bathsheba, arranged the death of her husband, and took her for his wife. He had adjusted to his iniquities and remained unrepentant. God, however, sent Nathan to him who spoke of a rich

man who had "very many flocks and herds" and a poor man who had "but one little ewe lamb." When a traveler arrived, the rich man refused to offer one of his flock, but took the poor man's lamb and prepared it for him. Infuriated by this tale, David, said, "As the Lord lives, the man who has done this deserves to die". Then, Nathan said to David, "You are the man". It was a painful moment of self-realization for David. "I have sinned against the Lord," said David, in an act of contrition. God was forgiving, but David did not escape punishment (2 Samuel, 12).

Saul, whose name was later changed to Paul, was on his way to Damascus seeking to imprison whatever Christians he might en-counter. Suddenly a brilliant flash of light from heaven struck him, knocking him to the ground. He heard the voice of Jesus speak to him: "Saul. Saul, why do you per-secute me?" "Who are you, Lord?" Saul asked. "I am Jesus," He replied, "whom you are persecuting". Saul was blinded by the light, but after three days of fasting and praying, something like scales fell from his eyes and he could see again. But Saul, now Paul and later St. Paul,

saw things in a different light. He could now recognize his former sins and the redeeming power of Christ (9: 1-19). He was liberated from the darkness of his sins and entered the light of Truth.

Aurelius Augustinus, by his own admission, was the most learned and the most dissolute student at the University of Carthage. Lust of the flesh had been his undoing. He was in his garden one day and in an agitated state. He was reading the Letters of St. Paul when he heard a child's voice saying *tolle lege, tolle lege* (take up and read). What Augustine read was a turning point in his life and led to his baptism. He opened the Bible at random and his eyes fell on Romans 13:13–14 which read: "Let us walk properly as in the daytime, not in orgies and drunkenness, not in sexual immorality and sensuality, not in quarreling and jealousy. But put on the Lord Jesus Christ, and make no provision for the flesh, to gratify its desires." Augustine abandoned his own sensuous ways and became a Christian, a bishop and a saint.

Ebenezer Scrooge is the central character of Charles Dicken's immortal classic, *A Christmas Carol*. His sin was that of avarice, more specifically described in the story as miserliness. He thought of nothing other than how much money he could save. He cared little for his employees and less for their families. In a harrowing sequence of events, he is visited by Jacob Marley, his former partner, and the ghosts of Christmas past, present and future. He is finally awakened to the fact that his miserliness is the cause of his misery and that life is to be enjoyed and happily shared with others. His conversion was a full 180 degrees. Early in the tale, he declared that:

> If I had my way, every idiot who goes around with
> Merry Christmas on his lips, would be boiled with his
> own pudding, and buried with a stake of holly through
> his heart. Merry Christmas? Bah humbug!

By the end of the story, he tells his readers that:

> I will honor Christmas in my heart, and try to keep it
> all the year. I will live in the Past, the Present, and the
> Future. The Spirits of all three shall strive within me. I
> will not shut out the lessons that they teach.

The examples from the Old Testament (King David), the New
Testament (St. Paul), the Fourth Century (St. Augustine), and
from the world of literature (Ebenezer Scrooge). Offer hope to
those who have difficulty coming to terms with their own sins.
Conversions, with the help of God and good friends, are possible.
Several doctors who performed abortions finally recognized the
horror of what they were doing and became pro-life Christians.
Sins need not be a permanent feature of one's character. Grace is
available and hope is always on the horizon.

The Seven Life-giving Virtues

The three theological virtues (faith, hope, and charity) plus the four cardinal virtues (prudence, justice, fortitude, and temperance) prove to be an effective array of weapons in combating the Seven Deadly Sins. But there is need for another brace of seven virtues that stand toe-to-toe with each of the deadly sins on an even level. Faith, hope, and charity are theological virtues, while the cardinal virtues belong to an earthly plane. I propose "Seven Life-giving Virtues," each one being both the antithesis and the antidote against each of their corresponding death-dealing vices. In this way, we can better understand the specific remedies for each of the deadly sins.

The opposite of pride is humility. Nikolai Berdyaev states that humility is "ontological". This means that humility is the virtue that perfectly corresponds to what man is in his being. To be oneself one must be humble. Pride is essentially unrealistic. It is, as G. K. Chesterton has remarked, "the falsification of fact by the introduction of self".

The humble person chooses realism over fiction, a seemingly easy choice, but he must ever guard against being proud of whatever humility he gains, which is assuredly not easy. Nonetheless, the humble person is well-armed to deal with the other deadly sins, each of which are fundamentally unrealistic.

Envy is sorrow at another's good fortune. Generosity springs from a loving heart and takes delight in the good which others have received. Envy spreads gloom; generosity brings a blessing to everything it touches. Generosity is life-giving in that it heartily welcomes all the good things that any person is fortunate enough to have.

Anger, being excessive, is contrary to justice. It disposes the angry person to hatred and violence. Patience is the strength of the heart that allows a person to retain his balance in the face of heated opposition. Patience quells anger and ensures that neither life nor limb is endangered. It is, therefore, a protector of life.

Both sloth and zeal are commonly misunderstood. Sloth is the reluctance or the refusal to involve oneself in anything of a spiritual nature. It is more pernicious than mere laziness. Zeal is not the narrowmindedness of the zealot. St. Paul advises us to "be zealous for spiritual gifts" (I Cor. 14:1). For St. Thomas Aquinas, zeal "arises from an intensity of love" (*Summa Theologica*, I-II, 28, 4). Zeal is enthusiasm for truth, justice, and life itself.

Lust is the preference for pleasure at the expense of the person. It uses, rather than respects the person. In this sense, it places the being of another at a lower level than pleasure, which is usually fleeting. Chastity is the logical and realistic antidote to lust. It is the virtue that brings the sexual appetite into harmony with reason. It is not the renunciation of sexuality, but its proper and reasonable use. Lust tends to overwhelm prudence and prevent a person from maintaining the self-possession he needs in order to be himself. Chastity is liberating.

Gluttony is the excessive use of food and drink. Temperance is the life-giving virtue that can prevent a person from the various forms of harm that this vice can bring about. The temperate person, because he is not ruled by his appetites, is more productive than his intemperate counterpart. He enjoys a certain serenity of spirit that serves him well in all his life's endeavors. Temperance is not simply moderation, but the virtue that holds the person together so that he can put forward his best efforts.

Avarice, or greed, is the desire to have far more than one needs. It is an appetite that has no logical limit. It grows on what it feeds, as Shakespeare warned in *Macbeth*. It does not know when there is "too much". But the "too much" can be personally ruinous. Gratitude is the virtue which allows us to give thanks for what we have. And in giving thanks, we appreciate what we have as well as what we need and, therefore, do not crave for what we do not need. Gratitude is the conqueror of greed. Furthermore, it is the benefactor of peace of mind.

In summary, the "Seven Life-giving Virtues" are humility (against pride), generosity (against envy), patience (against anger), zeal (against sloth), chastity (against lust), temperance (against gluttony), and gratitude (against avarice). The ensuing battle between virtue and vice is the drama and the outline of each individual's moral life as well as the story of man throughout the ages.

Let us note, finally, that it is futile to expect a virtue to arrive simply because a vice has been evicted. Roses do not grow simply because weeds have been removed. The elimination of any of the Seven Deadly Sins does not usher in a flowering virtue. Johnny Mercer's lyrics to a 1940's song

contains a bit of unexpected wisdom: "You got to accentuate the positive . . . latch on to the affirmative". Banishing the negative leaves a void. The only way to rid oneself of a vice and to ensure that it does not return, is to cultivate its corresponding virtue. The absence of a vice does not mean the presence of a virtue; but the presence of a virtue does mean the banishment of a vice.

We should begin our moral life by installing the Seven Life-affirming virtues which, by their very nature, will crowd out the Seven Deadly Sins.

The Fourth of July

The conflation of all the United States presidents into a homogenous and faceless "President's Day" is a disservice both to the American people as well as to the likes of Lincoln, Washington, Jefferson, and a few others who stood head and shoulders above the rest. Not all who held the country's highest office were equal in education, talent, dedication, and accomplishment. We should honor our more outstanding chiefs of state in a more individualistic manner.

America was truly blessed with the wisdom of a small coterie of extraordinary men who framed the Constitution and drafted the Declaration of Independence, which paid homage to God. The last sentence of the aforesaid document reads as follows:

> And for the support of this Declaration, with a firm Reliance on the Protector of divine Providence, we mutually pledge to each other our Lives, our Fortunes, and our sacred Honor.

The Founding Fathers were not averse to including God.

Was it a most unlikely coincidence or an act of divine Providence that America's second and third presidents—John Adams and Thomas Jefferson—died within hours of each other on July 4, 1826 on the 50th anniversary of the signing of the Declaration of Independence? And to stretch the notion of mere coincidence to its limit, James Monroe, the 5th president of the United States, also passed away on the Fourth of July (James Madison, America's 4th president, died on June 28, six days prior to July 4).

Another Fourth of July has a special but largely forgotten importance. In 1864, the Civil War was in full force. President

Lincoln was obviously preoccupied with grave concerns. General Grant's troops had been suffering massive casualties. In June of that year, a group of black men, residents of Washington, knocked on the door of the White House and presented a petition to the Commander in Chief. Security in 1864, it may be pointed out, was far more lax than it is today. Their spokesman, Gabriel Coakley, informed the President that he represented a group of Catholics who hoped to obtain permission to hold a lawn party on the White House grounds to raise money to build a Catholic church in Washington which would serve the black Catholic population in the nation's capital. Lincoln accepted the petition and ultimately gave it his signature. He told Coakley that he hoped the event would be a success.

And so, on July 4th, 1864, a strawberry festival was held on the White House lawn. Music was played and school children gave romantic and patriotic recitations. The gathering was a mixture of both black and white Catholics. The weather was cool and pleasant for that time of the year and approximately 1,500 people attended. Lincoln ensured the success of the event by attending in person along with his wife and most of his cabinet. The affair raised over $1,200, a large sum at that time, enough to build the church which was named after Martin De Porres, a lay

Dominican of African and Spanish descent who had been beatified three decades earlier. The new place of worship quickly attracted a large number of black Catholics, but also a sizable number of those who were white. A few years later, the church was replaced by Saint Augustine Catholic Church which continues to thrive until this day.

In that same year, 1864, on August 22, America's 16th president

gave an impromptu speech to a regiment of battle-weary soldiers on their way home after concluding their military service. His words were published in the press on the following day. As he explained to them:

> I happen, temporarily, to occupy this White House. I am living witness that anyone of your children may look to come here just as my father's child did. It is in order that each of you may have through this free government which we have enjoyed, an open field and a fair chance for your industry, enterprise and intelligence; that you may all have equal privileges in the race of life, with all its desirable human aspirations.

This part of Lincoln's address beautifully expresses his humility. He acknowledges how time is fleeting and that he will serve his country only "temporarily". But it also shows his commitment to a democratic way of life: "Anyone of your children" may become the president of the United States. And he alludes to the family in regarding himself as his "father's child" and to posterity in stating his hope that the democratic way will endure through time. And he conjoins a democratic government with giving each citizen the opportunity to do his best. Democracy and equality go hand in hand. This memorable and spontaneous address serves as a kind of x-ray of Lincoln's noble character.

American presidents have come from many different walks of life. Many were lawyers, but others were teachers, farmers, soldiers, governors, and congressmen. In addition, there was a haberdasher and a movie star. The faces of all the American presidents represent the diverse faces of all the American people.

February 12th is Lincoln's birthday. His stature and his contribution to America justify the entire month to be set aside as an appropriate way of honoring him. If there is a "President's Month," it belongs to the child of Nancy and Thomas Lincoln. George Washington is the father of his country, but Abraham Lincoln is its soul.

THE CONSEQUENCES OF OVERTURNING ROE V. WADE

The draft of a Supreme Court decision to overturn *Roe v. Wade* has been leaked to the press. This unprecedented disclosure of a future Supreme Court decision, however, is more like a dam burst than a leak. "We hold," writes Justice Samuel Alito, in Jeffersonian prose, "that *Roe v. Wade* must be overturned". In his 67-page statement, he goes on to state that:

> The Constitution makes no reference to abortion, and no such right is implicitly protected by any constitutional provision, including the one on which the defenders of *Roe* and *Casey* now chiefly rely.

If this apparent decision is confirmed this summer, what will be the consequences, we may ask? We can safely predict hysteria on the one hand, and rejoicing on the other. While no one has a crystal ball, we can reasonably anticipate what will likely happen. The word "likely" must be underscored, although reason can be a useful and reliable instrument. Four areas in particular may very well bring about positive results, despite the concerted efforts on the part of pro-abortionists to change the Court's ruling while complaining vociferously that their "rights" have been taken away.

1) Education: Once the hysteria dies down, it may become

clear to more people that the function of the Supreme Court is to interpret the Constitution and not to pander to specific interest groups. If a judicious reading of that document reveals that it contains no provision whatsoever for granting a woman a right to kill her unborn child, then *Roe v. Wade* must be overturned. It is far better to overturn *Roe v. Wade* than to turn the Court over to protest groups. The Constitution is the political

backbone of society. It gives society its enduring support and cohesiveness. Without such a backbone the country would fall into chaos, just as the human body, without its backbone, would fall apart.

2) Politics: The United States of America is a nation of citizens. These citizens, being a living part of their country, are not solo entities who are free to do anything they chose. They have rights, but they also have duties. The overturning of *Roe v. Wade* will not end abortion, but it most probably will reduce its number. This should be a boon for women and spare them the many adverse effects, both psychological and physical, that abortion brings about. Being a citizen of the United State confers many benefits and blessings. To be a citizen means honoring the laws of the land and respecting America's roots expressed in the *Declaration of Independence*, the *Gettysburg Address*, and other documents that honor the rights and dignity of all.

3) Sexuality: Abortion will lose status. One can no longer claim that abortion is a constitutionally protected right. This will lead many to understand that abortion and sexual activity are not to be regarded haphazardly as mere choices. Abortion can no longer be regarded as doing something "the American way". Some will begin to realize that sexuality has an intimate relationship with marriage and the family. Perhaps, with a better under-

standing of the negative implications of abortion, men will be more respectful of women and women will be more respectful of men. The unborn, indeed, are part of the human family.

4) Justice: It is a strange miscarriage of justice that the explicit statement in the *Declaration of Independence* that "all men are created equal" can give way to the nonsensical notion, as Justice Blackmun stated in *Roe v. Wade*, that the right to abortion is "implied in the penumbra" of the Constitution. His colleague on the bench, Byron White, was right when he characterized the *Roe* decision as, "an exercise in raw judicial power". He also criticized the Court majority for "interposing a constitutional barrier to state efforts to protect human life". Overturning *Roe* does take away from women the constitutional right to abortion. It means that such a right was never there in the first place. The regulation of abortion belongs not to the Supreme Court, but to the states. The late Justice Antonin Scalia remarked that:

> The permissibility of abortion and the limitations upon it, are to be resolved like most important questions in our democracy: by citizens trying to persuade one another and then voting.

According to Alito:

> It is time to heed the Constitution and return the issue of abortion to the people's elected representatives.

It should appeal to common sense that there would be no provision in any country's' Constitution for one person to take the life of an innocent person. Justice is not justice if it is not justice for all, including those human beings who are in the womb and tending toward birth. In reading the Preamble to America's Constitution, one is impressed by its dedication to unity and peace, and certainly not to division and violence.

> We the People of the United States, in order to form a more perfect Union, establish Justice, insure domestic

Tranquility, provide for the common defense, promote the general Welfare, and secure the Blessings of Liberty to ourselves and our Posterity, do ordain and establish this Constitution for the United States of America.

If *Roe v. Wade* is overturned, the American people will benefit, though these benefits will be denied by many who persist in opposing the very essence of their country as established by its Founding Fathers and concretized in its Constitution. Nevertheless, the recognition that the Constitution does not justify abortion is absolutely required if America is to fulfill its destiny as "one nation under God".

THE COURT AND COMMON SENSE

Common sense may not be chic in the eyes of the elite, but it provides a solid ground on which edifices can be mounted that will not crumble. We live in an age in which people pride themselves in being "progressive". But this fashionable term can mean abandoning one's roots in the interest of achieving something presumably better. Nonetheless, one cannot build a skyscraper without a firm foundation.

The late Antonin Scalia (1936- 2016), former Associate Justice of the United States Supreme Court, together with Bryan A. Garner, attend to this problem in their ground breaking book, *Reading Law: The Interpretation of Legal Texts* (2012). In the light of the chaos generated by the apparent overturning of *Roe v. Wade*, this 400-page volume is a welcomed antidote for the judicial activism that has caused more problems than it has solved. A few excerpts from the book provide its essential spirit and offer a corrective to the "liberal" interpretations that have gained fashion in the contemporary world of jurisprudence.

[W]e seek a return to the oldest and most common-sensical interpretive principle; in their full context words mean what they conveyed to reasonable people at the time they were written.

During the construction of St. Paul's Cathedral, the chief architect, Christopher Wren, took Britain's monarch on a tour. When the tour was completed, the monarch told the architect that he found it to be "amusing, awful, and artificial". Wren was not insulted because in seventeenth century England, these words meant, respectively, "amazing, awe-inspiring, and artistic". Words mean what they mean in the context of the time in which they were spoken. Scalia is a staunch advocate of "textualism".

"Since the mid-twentieth century, there has been a breakdown in the transmission of . . . [our] heritage". All we need to consider with regard to this point is the current cry of "cancel culture". I recall being on a live television show in Toronto. The audience consisted of high school students who were encouraged to make comments or criticisms. I had mentioned Martin Buber, made famous for his "I-Thou" philosophy. One student criticised me for referring to someone who is "dead". My critic spoke with  confidence, assuming he had the full support of his colleagues as well as contemporary society. Buber, of course, is part of our heritage and has had a decisive influence in theology, psychology, psychiatry, as well as in philosophy. My adolescent authority did not seem to realize that when a person dies, his thoughts do not necessarily die with him. As Walt Whitman has so beautifully stated:

So when a great man dies,
For years beyond our kin,
The light he leaves behind him lies
Upon the paths of men.

The distinguished lawyer, Arthur A. Schlesinger has remarked that "science and technology revolutionize our lives, but memory, tradition and myth frame our response". Society is in danger of losing the virtue of piety and respect for our ancestors and the treasures they have bequeathed us. "Over the past 50 years especially, we have seen the judiciary . . . take control of territory that ought to be settled legislatively".

As Justice Samuel Alito has stated:

> The Constitution makes no reference to abortion, and no such right is implicitly protected by any constitutional provision, including the one on which the defenders of *Roe* and *Casey* now chiefly rely.

In the same vein, Justice Scalia has stated that:

> The permissibility of abortion and the limitations upon it, are to be resolved like most important questions in our democracy: by citizens trying to persuade one another and then voting.

It should appeal to common sense that the United State Constitution does not provide a right for a mother to kill her unborn child, or that it has the authority to change the meaning of marriage.

"[S]ome commentators have claimed since the mid-20th century that all language is ambiguous". We consider how the literary fad known as "deconstruction" has rendered all words as "undecidable". A nadir, in this regard, was reached when former President Bill Clinton asked a questioner "What do you mean by 'is'?" One pundit claims that "words are merely vacuum capsules to be filled in by the listener". The Constitution consists in nothing but words. If language is essentially ambiguous and the meaning of words is undecidable, then the Constitution cannot possibly be interpreted. Likewise, the Bible has been deconstructed and no longer has either authority or force. It is utmost folly to think that Supreme Court Justices are required, by a solemn oath, to interpret something that is essentially uninterpretable. We have re-entered the Tower of Babel and do not know what we are talking about.

The proper interpretation of the constitution is critical, perhaps more critical than it has ever been. The consequence of culture losing sight of common sense, disparaging tradition, over-stepping legitimate boundaries, and rendering language ambiguous has had its effect on Supreme Court Justices. Antonin Scalia has been a national treasure. He has had the modesty to avoid judicial activism (more properly understood as "judicial recklessness") and to abide honorably and intelligently to what he has sworn to do, namely to interpret the Constitution.

Reading Law is a bit pricey, but it may be available at one's local library. One does not need to be a lawyer to appreciate the common sense richness of this splendid work. It is written for a broad audience, and the authors do not lack a sense of humor.

Domestic Tranquility

An important factor that has been ignored in the on-going discussion concerning the constitutionality of abortion is the Constitution's Preamble. While this important statement is part of the Constitution, it does not specify how the government should operate, but it does allude to its goals thereby providing a context for what the Founding Fathers were aiming to accomplish. The Preamble summarizes in a single, beautifully honed 52-word sentence, the basic purpose of the United States Federal government:

> We the People of the United States, in order to form a more perfect Union, establish Justice, insure domestic Tranquility, provide for the common defence, promote the general welfare, and secure the Blessings of Liberty to ourselves and our Posterity, do ordain and establish this Constitution for the United States of America.

I want to draw special attention in this article to the phrase "domestic Tranquility". These two words are open to two interpretations. The first relates to the country as a whole. It is only too obvious that abortion has been a source of bitter division and has set the stage for a veritable civil war on a moral plane. With regard to the family, abortion is, as a matter of fact, an instance of domestic violence. On either level, it is impossible to reconcile abortion with the notion of "domestic Tranquility" as specified in the Preamble of the Unites States Constitution.

C. Carolyn Graglia, who is a lawyer and a housewife, has written *Domestic Tranquility* (1998, 451 pages). Her book is clearly more in conformity with the *Preamble of the Constitution* than interpretations made by Supreme Court Judges who somehow find it congruent with abortion. Ms. Graglia argues, on the basis of considerable research, that the origin of modern feminism is rooted in the post-war exaltation of the marketplace combined with a dissatisfaction of domestic life. In this context, abortion, along with other abuses of human sexuality, has left marriage and the family in tatters. The ideal of domestic tranquility has been sadly replaced by the ideal of worldly success. The predictable result is domestic unhappiness.

Whatever one might say about abortion, it is evident that it does not bring about an atmosphere of tranquility. Abortion is a violent act. It is also a disordered one. "Peace is the tranquility of order," as St. Augustine has remarked. Abortion is a disruption of the natural order that proceeds from love to marriage to children to wise parenting. Abortion is not a conveyor of peace. It is not a blessing for either the present or for posterity. The aborted unborn enjoy neither the blessings of liberty nor a viable future.

"It is neither wealth nor splendor," Thomas Jefferson, America's third president, once remarked, "but tranquility and occupation which give you happiness". Tranquility has become, in the modern world, as elusive as peace and happiness. Abortion is the premature ending of a human life through violence. This violent act also weighs against the aborting woman, leading her in so many well documented cases, to bitter regret.

Domestic violence is a double edged sword. It has adverse effects on the domestic as well as the national level. Christopher Dawson, a historian who understood the importance of order, has stated in his book, *The Crisis of Western Education*, that:

> There is an obvious relation between the breakdown
> of the moral order and the breakdown of civilization
> when it loses its relation to the moral order.

Gross misinterpretations of the U. S. Constitution and disharmony in the home make for a lethal combination. Both in the home and abroad, domestic violence is approved and promoted. Yet the notion of domestic tranquility remains haunting. This is what people, in their heart of hearts, really want. It is one reason for naming the Apollo 11 landing site on the moon, "The Sea of Tranquility". But do we need to leave the planet to find this coveted ideal?

Domestic tranquility is what the Preamble promised. But this promise has been turned aside in favor of convenience and secular success. We domesticate cats and dogs while we "un-domesticate" the home. We should be kinder to ourselves than we are to stray dogs and homeless kittens. Not being able to find real tranquility, we become dependent on tranquilizers. For others, domestic tranquility means whiskey brewed and aged in one's own country. Abortion and tranquility are complete strangers. And, Supreme Court judges need not look elsewhere to discover the radical incompatibility between abortion and America's Constitution than to her Preamble.

Blessings and Curses

I once had the honor and pleasure, though only for a brief moment, of meeting Rabbi Yehuda Levin, an Orthodox Jew who is a fearless opponent of abortion. At the 25th March for Life, this wise "teacher" (which is what "Rabbi" means in English) delivered a strong message with Old Testamentary fury to the president of the United States:

> President Clinton! President Clinton, for once lead the country in the direction of respect for life, for God ordained life and morality. President Clinton! Moses said to Pharaoh, "Let my people go!" And we say to you today: Let our children grow! Let our children live!

Conscious of his orthodoxy and his fidelity to the Old Testament, I hoped I was not being impertinent when I suggested to him the one of the truly important duties of a rabbi is to help his people distinguish between blessings and curses. He did not disagree with me. New life is a blessing, while sin is a curse. Moreover, one will be cursed if he does not recognize and appreciate his blessings. Prior to the release of Kim Davis, the Kentucky county clerk imprisoned for refusing to issue same-sex "marriage" licenses., Rabbi Levin stated, "On a theological basis, I am

absolutely jealous of this woman, every minute she sits in prison to honor God's name she obtains an immense heavenly reward". In this case, Rabbi Levin was suggesting that Davis's prison sentence could be seen as a blessing. Indeed, God has implored us to recognize, difficult as it may be, the difference between blessing and curse, and to choose the former:

"I have set before you life and death, blessing and curse: therefore choose life, that both thou and thy seed may live" (Deuteronomy 30:19). Blessings have longevity from one generation to another.

Rabbi Levin is speaking to a world in which new life and moral responsibilities are often mistaken as curses while wealth, fame, and status are regarded as blessings. Life would be easier if blessings and curses did not come in disguises. Faith in God is needed so that blessings are appreciated for what they are. Our ego can get in the way of discerning the blessings that God makes available to us.

Sir Alec Guinness, a Catholic convert, recounts in his book, *Blessings in Disguise*, a most extraordinary event in which some-

thing that seemed clearly to be a blessing was, indeed, a curse. It was in the autumn of 1955 when he went to Los Angeles to make his first Hollywood film. While he and a companion were standing outside of a restaurant, "a fair young man in sweat shirt and blue jeans came running up to them and introduced himself as James Dean. "I'd like to show you something," he said, bursting with pride. "It's

126

just been delivered, I haven't even driven it yet." It was a sports-car with a large array of red carnations resting on the bonnet. Sir Alec, however, did not share Dean's enthusiasm for his shiny new vehicle. He said, in a "voice I could hardly recognize as my own, please, never get in it . . . If you get I that car you will be found dead in it by this time next week". Dean laughed at such an outrageous prediction. At four o-clock in the afternoon exactly one week later, James Dean was killed while driving that very car (pages 34-35).

The car, as it turned out, was not a blessing, but a curse. Guinness, himself was astonished by his antic-ipation of the tragic event. It is not always easy to distinguish blessing from curse. Was Beethoven's deafness a blessing in disguise because it allowed him to compose more undistractedly so that he could produce his monumental 9th symphony? Was Marilyn Monroe's fame and fortune a curse in disguise because it led to her untimely death at age 36? We need faith in Providence to recognize a blessing as a blessing, and a curse for what it

is. "We failed," said General Robert E. Lee, but in the good providence of God, apparent failure often proves a blessing". Humility helps us to recognize a blessing, while pride often sees a blessing as a curse. We choose what we think will be an unencumbered life. As a result, we shield ourselves from uninvited blessings while allowing self-made curses to gain control of our lives.

Bing Crosby crooned to us a timely message in the 1954 Hollywood hit, *White Christmas*:

> When I'm troubled and cannot sleep,
> I count my blessings instead of sheep,
> and I fall asleep counting my blessings.

Our problems can weigh upon our minds and make it difficult to be calm. The negative experiences can override the positive ones. We should not forget, our blessings, however, and accord them the primacy they deserve.

In *Sonnet 60*, the immortal bard reminds all of us of our mortality:

> Like as the waves make towards the pebbled shore,
> so do our minutes hasten to their end.

Time is running out for all of us. So critical, then, is the ability to recognize and put into practice our blessings, while recognizing but avoiding the curses that can ruin our lives. Rabbi Levin, Moses, Sir Alec Guinness, Robert E. Lee and, yes, even Bing Crosby have advice for us that we can take to heart: be humble, recognize and live by our blessings and keep curses from coming into our lives. Let he who is blessed bless (*Benedicat qui est benedictus*).

Our Two Most Popular Christmas Stories

The life of Christ is the greatest story ever told. But in terms of popularity, and thanks to television, our two most popular Christmas stories, that return to charm us each Christmas Season, are Charles Dickens' *A Christmas Carol* and Franks Capra's cinematic production of *It's a Wonderful Life*. The latter was inspired by Civil War historian, Philip Van Doren Stern's short story, *The Greatest Gift*, written in 1943. Charles Dickens published his masterpiece exactly 100 years earlier. A good story is a timeless gift to posterity.

Both stories rely on two factors that are essentially biblical. The first is based on the notion that time is not linear. The order of past, present, future, is altered so that the future can appear in the present to warn people of possible disasters that may take place in the future. The various prophets recorded in Sacred Scripture speak of future events that could be avoided by prayer and the avoidance of sin. Therefore Jacob Marley and other ghosts can arrive from the past to warn Ebenezer Scrooge of the disasters that lie ahead if he does not mend his ways. Clar-

ence Odbody, who is an angel, arrives from beyond time to save George Bailey from suicide.

The word "providence" (*pro + videre*) refers to the ability to see things before they happen. God is providential in this sense. He is not bound to the moment to moment sequence of temporal events. This providential character is essential to both stories and would lack credibility if they were not prepared for us by the Good Book. In contrast to this view is the fatalism that is beautifully, if not hopefully, recorded in Omar Khayyam's celebrated poem, *Rubaiyat*. In quatrain 71, we read the following:

> The Moving Finger writes, and, having writ,
> Moves on; nor all your Piety nor Wit
> Shall lure it back to cancel half a Line,
> Nor all your Tears wash out a Word of it.

In sharp contrast with the biblical view, the author sees nothing beyond the fixed succession of past-present-future. Nor does he envision the possibility of help from beyond. No one can arrive to help either Ebenezer Scrooge or George Bailey. They are grim victims of inexorable fate. Fatalism does not make for good stories even though Khayyam was able to frame it eloquently. Fate circumscribes us and deprives us of hope.

The second factor is associated with the principle that sin

must be avoided since "the wages of sin are death". Scrooge's sin is his implacable selfishness which is manifested in his extreme miserliness. George Bailey's sin is one of despair. He falsely believes that he is worth more, because of his insurance policy, dead than alive. Consequently, and at the end of his rope, he attempts to commit suicide. Selfishness and despair set in motion a chain of destruction. Scrooge is shown the gravestone marker that indicates the passing of Tiny Tim, George Bailey is shown how Bedford Falls has turned into Potterville, a world of sleazy entertainment, crime and corruption. Both characters are

horrified by this futuristic vision and are committed to changing their ways. They have been given, thanks to Divine Providence,

a clearer vision of the meaning of their lives that transcends time. This vision gives them a second chance, and they make the most of it. Selfishness and despair give way to sheer joy and a new appreciation of life.

We all like the idea of having a second chance, of being able to mend our ways, of gaining a clearer sense of the meaning of our life, and to realize, more sharply, that life is a wonderful gift that contains no end of opportunities to do good things. We relate to these stories on a personal level. In cheering for Scrooge and Bailey, we are cheering for ourselves at the same time. And then it may occur to us that this is the basic message of Christmas: love of neighbor, release from fear, and joy at the arrival of Christ in a manger in Bethlehem.

> God rest ye merry gentlemen,
> let nothing you dismay,
> remember Christ our Savior
> was born on Christmas Day.

THE MOST
DANGEROUS PLACE
FOR AN AFRICAN AMERICAN
IS IN THE WOMB.
THATSABORTION.COM

Other Titles by Dr. DeMarco

Abortion in Perspective

Sex and the Illusion of Freedom

Today's Family in Crisis

The Anesthetic Society

The Shape of Love

The Incarnation in a Divided World

In My Mother's Womb

Hope for a World Without Hope

Chambers of the Heart

How to Survive as a Catholic in a Parochial World

Character in a Time of Crisis

The Many Faces of Virtue

Timely Thoughts for Timeless Catholics

New Perspectives in Contraception

The Integral Person in a Fractured World

Patches of God-Light

The Heart of Virtue

Virtue's Alphabet from Amiability to Zeal

Biotechnology and the Assault on Parenthood

Architects of the Culture of Death

Being Virtuous in a Non-Virtuous World